DOWN HOME WIT & WISDOM

STEVE CHAPMAN

HARVEST HOUSE PUBLISHERS
EUGENE, OREGON

Cover design by Writely Designed, Buckley, Washington

DOWN HOME WIT AND WISDOM
Copyright © 2015 by Steve Chapman
Published by Harvest House Publishers
Eugene, Oregon 97402
www.harvesthousepublishers.com

Library of Congress Cataloging-in-Publication Data
    Chapman, Steve.
    Down home wit and wisdom / Steve Chapman.
       Pages cm
    ISBN 978-0-7369-6352-7 (pbk.)
    ISBN 978-0-7369-6353-4 (eBook)
    1. Christian life—Anecdotes. 2. Life skills—Anecdotes. 3. Aphorisms and apothegms.
    4. Chapman, Steve—Ethics. I. Title.
    BV4517.C45 2015
    248.4—dc23

                         2014050051

Printed in the United States of America

      15 16 17 18 19 20 21 22 23 / VP-CD / 10 9 8 7 6 5 4 3 2 1

To my dear wife, Annie.
Without you, I'd still be
staring at a blank screen.

Acknowledgments

All of my thanks goes to my dear wife, Annie, who spent many hours helping me compile the hundreds of bits of wisdom from which these quips were chosen. Her depth of insight about life and how to live it successfully not only was a main contributor to this book, but it has made a lasting and loving difference in everyone around her, including family and friends…and especially me.

Contents

★

Simple Words, Profound Truth

There is hardly anything more exciting than encountering a bit of wisdom that generates a positive change in the way I live and how I think. When it happens, I know that the light of truth gets a little brighter in my mind and the darkness occupied by doubt, confusion, anxiety, and fear must yield to it.

Most of the life-altering insights that have impacted me have not come in lofty language, hard-to-understand concepts, or long, drawn-out explanations. Instead, many of them are found in simple words that reveal profound truths that are easy to grasp. Better yet, they're very often contained in quips that would fit on a bumper sticker.

Down Home Wit & Wisdom is a collection of my favorite brief-but-beneficial insights. I offer them to you not just because they have the potential to change your life for the better, like they have mine, but because I suspect you may be as hungry as I am for the common sense they contain.

Along with each memorable quip, I've included a short story to illustrate how the wisdom applies to real-life situations. In some stories, the names of the individuals have been changed for the sake of privacy, but their experiences were very real.

In regard to the origin of the quips, some I've heard from others, and whenever possible, I've given credit to whom credit is due. Others are just out there in our world, accepted as general wisdom. Some of them are products of my personal discoveries and are in my own words.

There is a reality I must admit: Because there is nothing new under the sun, you may have already thought of some of them or heard some of them before in one form or another. If so, let's just consider it a case of "great minds running together," okay?

I'm thankful that you've chosen to spend some time with me through these pages. I hope you enjoy the down-home style of these time-tested truths. I especially hope they serve to make your life more enjoyable.

Steve Chapman

1

"Don't Shoot the Horse You're Ridin' On"

I've had some endurance-testing experiences in my years, including running marathons, riding a bicycle for several hundred miles, and remaining at full-draw with my compound bow long enough to out-wait the keen eyes of a huge bull elk. But of all the things that have tried my perseverance, one that was even more challenging than these was helping my children maintain a right attitude while traveling.

My wife, Annie, and I are Christian musicians, and we've traveled all over the United States putting on concerts, sharing the gospel of Jesus Christ, and offering families hope and encouragement. For many years, when our kids were growing-up, we took them on the road with us. Being gifted musically, Heidi and Nathan often worked alongside us.

However, an area that required the occasional pressing of our kids' "attitude reset" button was in the area of public relations. It usually happened following a concert. When an evening ended, our usual activity was to go to the lobby of the venue and spend time meeting and greeting folks who had made the effort to attend the event.

Once in a while, when our kids experienced a long day of travel, helped with equipment setup, rehearsed, and participated in the concert, when it came time to head to the lobby after dismissal, I noticed their demeanor wouldn't be quite as sociable as I thought it should be. Very often my impressions were confirmed afterward when we were on the way to our lodging. They'd complain about having to answer the all-to-familiar questions, such as "What about your schooling?" and "Are your parents really in love?"

I fully understood the challenge our kids faced to keep smiling as they interacted with people, but I wanted them to also know that our entire family needed to be cordial with folks for two good reasons. First, the messages in our songs were offered to encourage and build up individuals and families who came to hear us. The folks were important enough to greet with friendly demeanors when we talked one-on-one with them. In addition, God was gracious enough to not only allow us to do the work we did, but He also chose to use our gifts as a way to supply the funds we needed to fill our bread bin and butter dish. With these reasons in mind, before the evening was over I would often give our two road companions a pep talk.

> Kids, you did a good job tonight. Thanks for being here with us. Just a reminder about the people we talk to after our concerts—they make a lot of effort to be here, they spend hard-earned cash to get tickets, they buy gas for their vehicles, and some of them use their precious family funds to pick up our CDs. Don't forget they deserve our best treatment. I'll say it one more time: Don't shoot the horse you're ridin' on!

Our teens didn't seem to resent me reminding them that the people who had been in the chairs at the concert were precious to us. I greatly appreciated their willingness to hear me out and take in the message.

The era of traveling with our son and daughter is well behind us now. Today their lives are wall-to-wall busy with being mates to their spouses, raising our GrandChaps, working, and doing the things parents do. They both have responsibilities that include dealing with the public. I'm happy to report that they're handling their situations very well. But like everyone, their good attitudes are sometimes tested by exhaustion or, worse, by challenges brought about by unkind or insensitive comments.

When they share those experiences, I can't help but think that very possibly one of the reasons they remain successful is that somewhere in the back of their minds they hear the echoes of truth from the wisdom phrase "Don't shoot the horse you're ridin' on." If so, my speech-making was not in vain.

> To enjoy your work and accept your lot in life—this is indeed a gift from God (Ecclesiastes 5:19 NLT).

"Sometimes You Have to Listen with Your Eyes"

Through the years of writing songs to offer at our family-oriented concerts, one subject we've often addressed is the father/child relationship. We've found that this topic generates both smiles and tears.

The smiles on the faces in the audience usually indicate the folks had good experiences with their dads. The tears, however, tell us that somewhere along the way something happened that caused them to have to deal with negative emotions, such as sadness, disappointment, anger, and even fear regarding their relationships with their fathers.

Of all the painful feelings that sons and daughters talk about when we've spoken with them after concerts, there is one that seems to be mentioned most often. Through misty eyes they've shared how much they wished they would've *heard* their dads say the words "I love you."

As Annie and I speak to folks who long to hear those words, we've discovered that in many cases their fathers were good dads who took good care of their children. But the dads simply weren't verbal with their love. When this is the situation, we gently remind them that there is another way to hear "I love you" than with just their ears. With all the compassion we can muster, we say, "Sometimes you have to listen with your *eyes*."

To help them understand what we mean, we quote or sing our song "Love Was Spoken."

Love Was Spoken

Before the sun came up, Daddy rolled out of bed
He'd go to work, and that's how love was said
He'd spend the money that he made all week
To feed a hungry family
That's how love would speak

Oh, love was spoken
Though Daddy rarely used the words
Love was spoken
In everything he did
Love was all we heard

On Saturday morning when a man ought to rest
Dad would work on the house, and that's how love was said
When Sunday came, we were off to the chapel
Love was spoken so pure and tender

Saying love did not come easy
But we did not criticize
'Cause we could hear him say he loved us
When we'd listen with our eyes

Oh, love was spoken
Though Daddy rarely used the words
Love was spoken
In everything he did
Love was all we heard[1]

"The Bobber Won't Bounce If It Ain't in the Water"

I'd never heard anyone play the piano as well as my friend. There was a unique smoothness about his keyboard technique that created music that touched the very core of my soul and left me begging to hear more when he stopped. His ability was amazing, indeed, but what was even more amazing to me was how hesitant he was to go beyond his living room with his musical skills. I told him more than once that if I could play like he did, I'd find a way to turn the black and white keys into some green cash.

I won't forget the day I suggested that he pitch his playing to some studios that hired musicians for recording-session work. His response revealed his apprehension. He put his hands in his pockets and sort of shuffled his feet. His reaction told me that the thought of playing publically and asking to be paid for it made him very nervous.

However, while his body language said one thing, the look in his eyes said another. He gazed past me with a half-grin, seeming to be looking far away. I wondered if in his mind he was seeing himself working on Music Row in Nashville. Assuming that he really did long for the chance to play outside his small circle of friends and family, I offered him a friendly bit of advice taken from my experience as an angler: "Buddy, the bobber won't bounce if it ain't in the water!" He caught on quickly. He knew I was saying no one was going to bite on his expert piano playing until he went fishing for some opportunities to make it known.

> When you praise someone privately they feel
> good about themselves. When you praise
> someone publicly they feel good about you.
> **Steve and Annie Chapman**

About six months went by. One day I got an invitation in the mail to attend an event sponsored by a company I wasn't familiar with. As I looked at it and wondered why I would receive it, I saw a name I recognized. Under the words "Featuring the music of…" was my friend's name! It was his first gig as a guest musician. He sent the invitation to let me know that "the bobber had bounced" and he'd gotten a bite.

The "bobber in the water" truth not only applies to instrumentalists like my friend. There are countless others who can benefit by it, including songwriters, athletes, engineers, mathematicians, teachers, aviators, accountants, chefs, and authors, to name a few. If you have a talent you long to offer to others but you're afraid to make it known, I say, "It's time for you to go fishing!" Go ahead and drop the bait into the waters of opportunity. Until you do, you'll never know the exciting joy of seeing the bobber bounce.

Cast your bread on the surface of the waters, for you will find it after many days (Ecclesiastes 11:1).

4

"The Hungrier You Are, the Harder You'll Hunt"

I was watching a golf tournament on TV one Saturday afternoon, and I was especially interested in the progress of one of the younger players. As the youthful golfer stood over a putt on the eighteenth green, the commentator quietly spoke and reminded the viewing audience that we were watching a player who was in contention for his first win on the PGA circuit. If he birdied the hole, he would go to the clubhouse only one shot behind the leader. He'd have good momentum for Sunday's final round.

The silence was intense as the putt was made. The gallery moaned as the ball barely missed the hole and stopped a couple of inches beyond. After tapping in for par, the player retrieved his ball, tipped his hat to the crowd, shook his fellow competitors' hands, and headed for the clubhouse to sign his card.

But he wasn't finished for the day. With part of the focus for the broadcast turned to the young golfer's quest for putting his name in the book of winners, a cameraman followed him after he left the clubhouse. The golfer carried a large bucket of balls and headed to the practice range. The announcer noted that the ambitious golfer would likely spend half-an-hour to an hour on the range and about the same amount of time on the practice putting green before leaving.

Hunt with your kids when they're young so you
won't have to hunt for them when they're older.

Author unknown

Annie joined me on the couch to watch the drama. As they were showing a few practice drives, she asked how long 18 holes of golf takes to play.

I answered, "Three to four hours on average."

She said, "You'd think he'd had enough golf for one day."

That's when I reminded her that "the hungrier you are, the harder you'll hunt."

There was a ravenous appetite for success in the heart of that young golfer that drove him to stay and practice. This same level of hunger is found outside the boundaries of the fairways as people pursue their dreams and goals. There are singers wanting record deals, lawyers wanting to win cases, salespeople who have the number one spot on the chalkboard as their goal, boxers who have championship titles in their sights, cooks who long to wear tall white hats, and hunters who want their names in the record books. These are just a few examples of those who are on quests, whose hunger compels them to stay in the hunt.

I was glued to the TV on Sunday afternoon as I watched the young golfer fight his nerves and win the tournament on the first hole of a sudden-death playoff. It was exciting to watch...as well as inspiring. So much so that I asked myself, "What am I hungry for?"

We also have as our ambition, whether at home or absent,
to be pleasing to [the Lord] (2 Corinthians 5:9).

5

"Maintaining a Happy Marriage
Is a Matter of Math"

When our children were traveling and singing with us, from time to time someone would pull one of them aside after the concert and quietly ask, "Are your parents really as happy as they seem?" The question implied doubt that we (or any other couple, for that matter) could actually enjoy marriage.

When our children answered with a confident, "Yes, they are!" it's likely the inquirers walked away believing Annie and I had brainwashed our kids. But the truth is, we are happy together. We've been married more than 40 years now, and we're still going strong. I'm sure that one of the reasons for our happiness is that we approach our relationship mathematically. What do I mean? One of our road trips explains how all four basic math functions help our relationship be a pleasure.

Annie and I took off from Tennessee and headed to Illinois for a Friday-night concert that was to start at seven o'clock. Our sound check was scheduled for four o'clock that afternoon, so we left our driveway early enough to allow us to arrive at our lodging place around three to freshen up. The paper documents I had in my folder said the sponsoring organization was in Lincoln, Illinois, which is about 40 miles north of Springfield. So, six-and-a-half hours later, when we were nearing Lincoln, I keyed in the street of the hotel on our GPS. Oddly enough, the street came up in Springfield, which was 40 miles *behind* us.

Bewildered, I dug the papers out of my folder to call the sponsor and ask for directions. That's when I noticed in the middle of the page that the concert location was *Springfield* instead of Lincoln. I couldn't control the shock. I involuntarily groaned aloud and muttered, "Oh, shucks!" My reaction alerted Annie that something was wrong.

"What's the problem?" she asked.

I didn't respond immediately because I dreaded to break the news to her that I had made such a directional blunder. I finally spoke up and confessed. In that moment, she chose to *multiply* kindness. Her words were soothing and showed a lot more mercy than I deserved.

"Well, I know you didn't intentionally drive *80 miles* out of our way just to add to how tired we are."

I noted the emphasis she'd put on the extra mileage on our bodies, but I also noticed that she'd *subtracted* judgment by not adding something like, "It's already three o'clock! We're going to have to go straight to the church instead of stopping at the hotel. Obviously you don't care that I'm not going to get to wash my hair before we go to the church." Or she could have offered a shorter version: "You're an idiot!" I appreciated her grace and forgiveness.

We arrived at the church about 15 minutes late. We knew our window for completing the sound check in time to share dinner at five o'clock with the staff of the sponsoring group was smaller than we'd planned. For that reason, we both hit the pavement running and went into "*dividing* the work" mode. Annie set up the product table with our books and CDs, and I hit the stage to do the technical stuff.

We *added* humor to the mix the next morning during our drive home. We enjoyed several miles of laughter as we talked about what our trip might have looked like from an aerial point of view. If someone had filmed us from a drone, they would have seen us leave our house in Tennessee, drive 430 miles on a 390-mile trip, flip-flop at an Interstate exit, drive back 40 miles, jump out of our van, get set up, and then try to act like nothing happened in front of a crowd of folks who wanted to hear some music and thoughts on how to have a better marriage.

To *sum* up, in marriage if you *multiply* kindness, *subtract* judgment, *divide* the work, and *add* humor, you'll reap the *dividend* of happiness. Yep! Maintaining a happy marriage is a matter of math!.

"True Character Is Who You Are When Everyone Is Looking"

Consider the following hypothetical situation.

Imagine that you just happened to be walking by a crowd of demonstrators gathered in the town square in support of legislation to ban abortion. While you strongly agree with their mission, you aren't the type to hold a sign, wear a statement T-shirt, or yell through a bullhorn for the sake of publicly letting your convictions be known.

Across the street is another group of people with views completely opposite of yours. The volume of their collective voices in resistance to the abortion ban is even greater than that of the pro-lifers.

Even though you support the pro-life group and whisper a prayer for them as they bravely stand firm on the side of the unborn, your intent is to walk on by without getting involved. You come to the corner of the block and start across the intersection. About halfway to the other side, when you're right between the two groups of activists, out of nowhere a man with a microphone and a cameraman step into your path. Startled, you look at the interviewer for a moment with a stunned expression on your face.

"I'm from News Channel 6," he says. "Why did you come here today, and what side of the abortion issue are you on."

A few seconds pass that feel like hours. You notice that the crowd noise has significantly faded. As if cued by a movie director, people within earshot seem to stop what they're doing and lean in to hear what you have to say to the viewing audience that likely numbers in the tens of thousands.

What will you do? Will you look into the camera and speak the convictions you quietly hold? Or will you stay silent and cave under the fear of being publically outed as an individual who believes in the sanctity of life?

That's what is meant by the wisdom statement, "True character is who you are when everyone is looking."

Sanctify Christ as Lord in your hearts, always being ready to make a defense to everyone who asks you to give an account for the hope that is in you, yet with gentleness and reverence (1 Peter 3:15).

"Be Better Than Your Old Self"

Doing better than someone else's best is not as satisfying
as doing better than your best.

When I turned 30, I bought a cheap pair of tennis shoes and
started running for the sake of strengthening my heart and
getting rid of some accumulation around my waistline. I'd never been
a runner prior to that year. Because I immediately enjoyed it, it didn't
take long to work my way up to three miles a day.

About six months into my newfound, health-enhancing hobby, I
saw an ad for a 5 kilometer (5K) race in a town south of where we lived.
Just for the experience, I decided to enter and sent in my $20 fee. When
race day came, I was pumped, trained, carbed up, and well equipped
with some high-dollar shoes and fancy lightweight shorts and jersey. I
had visions of taking home a trophy.

Because I hadn't been a race participant before, I wasn't acquainted
with the type of people who would be there. When I drove up to the
event site and saw a lot of lean, long-legged guys and gals doing their
prerace warm-up stretching, I realized that my dream of accepting
some post-race hardware had to be put back to bed.

When the starting horn sounded, I took off and felt good. The
three-and-a-tenth-mile course was only slightly hilly, and the temper-
ature was a comfortable 75 degrees. About 28 minutes later, I could
see the finish line in the distance. There were so many others who were
ahead of me that I decided to put my body and mind on cruise control and just enjoy my first run with an actual race number pinned on

my jersey. However, something happened at that point in the competition that was self-incriminating and, to be honest, quite embarrassing.

When I was about 300 yards from the colorful, flag-lined finishing tunnel, I heard the sound of tennis shoes pounding the pavement next to me. I could tell by the pace of the footsteps that I was about to be passed. When we were side-by-side, I saw that the runner was a female. Initially it didn't bother me that a lady was going to go by me, but with each stride toward the finish line the volume of my male-ego-driven protest rose in my mind. Not many seconds later I silently admitted how I really felt. *I can't let that woman pass me right here near the finish line. Too many eyes are on us. Man, it's time to kick it into high gear if you want to save face.*

With total disregard for how obvious it was that I would turn into a running chauvinist in order to beat the lady to the finish line, I put my head back like the guy in the movie *Chariots of Fire* and slammed the pedal to the metal.

When I crossed the line I was about 10 yards ahead of the female. I was gasping for air as I stopped. I bent over and put my shaking hands on my knees. After about five seconds of recovery I stood straight and looked around. That's when I realized what an idiot I'd been. Other runners and a couple of race staffers were staring at me, as if saying, "Seriously? Are you happy now?"

If you see a sign along the highway that says,
"Scenic Overlook," ignore it and look anyway.

Steve Chapman

I walked wobbly-legged through the finish area to get my little ribbon and then went to my car. I knew there was no need to hang around for the trophy presentation.

As I drove home, I felt more than sore muscles. I had an ache in my ego for having shown such an "I won't let a girl beat me" attitude. Until I got a few more races under my shoes, I didn't realize that the best way to feel good after a race (and keep some dignity) is to not try to be beat the next runner but to try beating my previous race time.

That mindset has served me well in other situations too. For instance, as a songwriter my goal now is not to write a song better than any other writer, but to write a song better than the last one I wrote. I'm amazed at how much more enjoyable and productive the process is.

"Courtesy for Cash Means Strings Attached"

We Can All Do Better Than That

You get a franchise smile with your coffee at the
    drive-through
When you're gettin' off the plane you get a company,
    "Thank you!"
Everybody seems so nice as long as you're givin' 'em cash
But we can all do better than that

Here's a smile; it's free
Here's a wink; it's on me
Here's my wish that the world would treat you nice
    with no strings attached
We can all do better than that

That little piece of candy on your hotel pillow…
It's management school
That pat on your back with your brand-new car…
It's a company rule
And that hand ain't just for shakin' after it carries
    your bags
But we can all do better than that

Here's a smile; it's free
A thumbs up; it's on me
Here's my wish that the world will treat you nice
    with no strings attached
Oh, we can all do better than that

Bein' nice is just good business; I know it's true
But if you need some nice and you're out
    of cash, I've got a deal for you

Here's a smile; it's free
A high-five; it's on me
And here's my wish that the world would treat you nice
    with no strings attached
Oh, we can all do better than that[2]

Remind your people to…be gentle and truly courteous to
all (Titus 3:1-2 TLB).

"Being Needed Is Almost as Good as Being Wanted"

Being wanted by someone is a longing that runs deep in all humans. Usually that desire is fulfilled simply because of who we are to others and not because of what we can do for them. A son or daughter, for example, can enjoy the feeling of being wanted by parents based solely on the fact that he or she is "bone of their bone and flesh of their flesh." Nothing other than being born and breathing is usually required of the child to receive the comforting awareness that they're wanted.

Unfortunately for some people, the closest they can get to feeling wanted by someone is *to be needed* by someone. Because they're resigned to the belief that "being needed" is almost as good as "being wanted," they jump at every chance to do something for others. Such is the case for the girlfriend in this story song:

Needed

He calls me and tells me that he needs me
He tells me that he's lonely…says, "Can I come right now?"
And so
I'll go
Even though I understand
That it's more about what I can do than who I am

So I get in my car
Make the drive—it's not that far

'Cause missing just one chance to be with him
Is something I'd regret
It's not the best way to be treated
But I'll take being needed
'Cause it's as close to being wanted as it gets

So I'll go to him and hope someday he'll see
To be loved is to be wanted; that's all I need[3]

The accommodating girlfriend in the lyric may sound emotionally weak, but the truth is she's showing some strength of character that can be admired. By accepting the reality that being needed is almost as good as being wanted, she is able to be at peace with her situation. The same peace can be found in others who have also concluded that being needed is a close cousin to being wanted.

Never argue harshly with a friend. You may win
the argument, but you may lose your friend.

Author unknown

There are spouses who willingly do things for their mates because they know it contributes to their partners wanting their presence. There are grandmothers who gladly break their backs to take care of grand-kids in order to sense that their grown child (or perhaps their in-law) desires their company. There are also friends who do a ton of things for a friend in order to enjoy just an ounce of feeling wanted.

Perhaps you recognize yourself as a person who willingly does things for someone so that the person's want for you increases. If so, you have my respect for showing such a strong resolve. After all, it resembles what happened at the cross of Christ. He knows that some-times we need Him more than we want Him.

God demonstrates His own love toward us, in that while
we were yet sinners, Christ died for us (Romans 5:8).

"A Great Man Fights for Freedom Even When He Knows He Might Not Live to Enjoy It"

How grateful all of us should be for those who have died in wars while defending our nation's liberty and safety. In an effort to honor these heroes, my friend Lindsey Williams and I penned this lyric.

Took a Bullet For

I watched him struggle across the Mall there in Washington
He had come to speak to an old friend who had fallen
 back in World War II
They were right out of high school
He looked across that Field of Stars and started talking
He said, "Luke, do you remember ol' Ike?"
He said the whole world is watching our great crusade
"Man it seems like it was yesterday day when…

"Everybody pledged life, love, and honor to the red, the
 white, and the blue
And we fought for liberty and justice for all like it was gos-
 pel truth
We were one nation under God on that beach back in '44
That's the America you gave your life to and I took a bullet for"

He said, "Luke, every step I take reminds me of Normandy
'Cause I carry around a piece of lead that they couldn't take
    out of me
Lord knows it hurts, but let me tell you what's worse…
In our schools and government, and even in our houses of
    prayer
What's wrong and right ain't black and white like it was
    when we went over there
Too many shades of gray
You know I wish I was back in the day when…

"Everybody pledged life, love, and honor to the red, the
    white, and the blue
And we fought for liberty and justice for all like it was gos-
    pel truth
We were one nation under God on that beach back in '44
That's the America you gave your life to and I took a
    bullet for"

I stepped up to him and said, "Excuse me, sir. I'd like to
    shake a hero's hand
I know you feel there ain't many of us left, but let me tell
    you where I stand…

"I'm proud to pledge life, love, and honor to the red, the
    white, and the blue
'Cause I believe in liberty and justice for all, just like you
And we're one nation still needing God like we did back
    in '44
That's the America Luke gave his life to,
And that's the America that I thank God you
Took a bullet for" [4]

Greater love has no one than this, that one lay down his life
for his friends (John 15:13).

"A Clean Barn Means Nothin's Goin' On at the Farm"

Whenever people come to our house unannounced and walk into our kitchen, more than likely they'll see disorder on the table. There are usually a couple of laptops we use for writing books, composing song lyrics, as well as maintaining our website (www.Steveand AnnieChapman.com). They might see stacks of papers around the salt and pepper shakers, an unfinished cup of cold coffee, and an empty granola bar wrapper. It's a sight that my organized wife would rather have time to clear before company shows up, but when we're caught off guard by visitors, she doesn't apologize. Instead, she usually says, "Hey, it's a working ranch around here."

The explanation for why our kitchen table lacks neatness is rooted in a biblical proverb: "Where no oxen are, the manger is clean, but much revenue comes by the strength of the ox" (Proverbs 14:4). We know that if our "barn" stayed uncluttered, it would mean that nothing productive was happening. For that reason we're very grateful to have the work to do that our piled-up kitchen table represents.

While we use our paraphrase of the proverb to help our visitors understand and appreciate the disarray they see, there is yet another version of the verse we use to comfort each other. Specifically, it happens after we've hosted our rambunctious grandchildren overnight.

If you want to be with your kids, take 'em fishin'.
If you want to go fishin', don't take the kids.

Steve Chapman

While we totally enjoy our GrandChap sleepovers, the debris field left behind by their explosive energy is admittedly not easy to clean up, especially while they're still awake. Knowing better than to do room restoration while the "toddlernados" are still ripping through our house, we wait until after they're in bed, prayers are said, and they're tucked in.

Very often as we're on our hands and knees scraping up the toy parts, residual mac and cheese and O's of oats, and the remnants of arts and crafts, one of us will comfort the other with "A clean barn means nothin's goin' on at the farm."

The revised paraphrase of the proverb brings a smile for a good reason. Just like our cluttered kitchen table tells our company that our house is still a productive, working ranch, the "grand" mess we see on our floors is glorious evidence of the joyous fact that life is still going on in our barn. We wouldn't have it any other way. Can you relate?

"Test Your Children's Social Skills by Inviting Friends Over During TV Time"

One moment that my parents put in the "I wish Steve hadn't said that" file took place when I was a mere five years old. They'd invited a couple to come to our house for dinner, and after the meal and dessert were served, my folks asked their guests to stay a while and visit.

My sister and I joined the adults in the living room and quietly listened to their conversation. I may have appeared outwardly content to just sit on the couch next to our visitors, but inside I was growing more anxious by the minute. Though I was only five, I knew that the hour my favorite TV show would come on was approaching fast.

The 30-minute broadcast was called *The Adventures of Superman*. I lived from week-to-week in anticipation of seeing the man in the long cape fly across the TV screen. I was such a Superman junkie that I'd memorized the opening. I can still hear it today!

Announcer: Kellogg's, the greatest name in cereal, presents *The Adventures of Superman*. Faster than a speeding bullet. More powerful than a locomotive. Able to leap tall buildings in a single bound.

People on the street: "Look, up in the sky! It's a bird! It's a plane! It's Superman!"[5]

As I sat and endured the adults droning on and on without any concern whatsoever that Clark Kent was about to face another bad man and save a life or two, I grew really antsy. My arms were folded and my legs, which were not long enough to reach the floor yet, were shaking side-to-side with frustration. Finally, I couldn't take it anymore. With a voice that must have had some very pronounced pout about it, I looked at my lap and mumbled, "Why don't you all go home so I can watch television!"

My intent was for only our company to hear, but in my exasperation I'd unfortunately said it loudly enough for *everyone* in the room to hear…including my parents. Conversation suddenly came to a dead-air halt.

After a few seconds of silence, I dared look up at my mother. I recognized the ire in her eyes. The red on her face was frightening. My dad uncrossed his legs, grabbed the arms of his chair, and leaned forward as he cleared his throat. I'd seen him react that way before—usually when I'd provoked him with my unruly behavior. I instantly knew my life was about to end.

I glanced at my sister with hopes of finding some comfort in her face. I noticed a slight smile, but I couldn't tell if she was happy that *I* had "invited" our company to leave so she could watch *Superman* too or if she was glad that I would be the one to suffer the doom that was sure to come.

My parents apologized for their son's unacceptable request, and their friends assured them they were not offended. They continued visiting. I noticed that I was not asked to go to my room (where I would worry and wait for the physical punishment I knew was coming). Instead, I stayed on the couch.

In retrospect, it was the perfect punishment. Across from me on the opposite side of the room was our Zenith TV. The face of it remained solid black, and the speaker was totally silent as the big hand and little hand of the clock on the wall to my right reached the time for the show to start. I was beyond miserable knowing that Superman had just jumped through the window and was off to conquer evil without me.

While my parents didn't intend to perform a test of my social skills that evening, they did discover a way to get a good reading on them. It's a method that all parents who own televisions and popular electronic devices that kids like could consider. If you do, and your testing reveals a bend in your child's basic understanding of social skills, such as courtesy, you can also do what my folks did to straighten me out. They didn't resort to spanking. Instead, they did something far more painful and memorable. They made sure the TV was off on the nights that *The Adventures of Superman* aired. It was at least four *long* weeks before I was allowed to watch my show again. I was grateful for the chance to reconnect with the man who flew, but looking back I'm a lot more thankful that I learned a really important lesson that has lasted a lifetime.

As a result of my parents' wise correction, I will never ask you to leave if you're visiting at our house when my favorite TV show is about to air (*The Andy Griffith Show* of the black-and-white era). And it won't be because there's a recording device attached to the television, I promise.

13

"Change the Unacceptable; Accept the Unchangeable"

I don't have to go far at all to show that finding peace of mind sometimes requires changing the unacceptable or accepting the unchangeable. Both illustrations are readily available in my head.

For "changing the unacceptable," I offer my teeth as an example. I didn't like how they looked, but I also didn't realize how little I liked their appearance until I saw them in profile on my TV screen. I was the guest on an outdoor show that featured me and my compound bow on a deer hunt. The cameraman held steady on a big eight-pointer as I took the shot. He filmed a perfect hit and then followed the whitetail as it ran about ten yards and toppled over.

I sat next to the cameraman and started to wildly celebrate. That's when the man turned the camera on me. He filmed me as I ripped my camo head net off and smiled wide while looking at the heavy buck lying within sight of the treestand.

It wasn't until after the footage was edited and the show aired that I saw the hunt for the first time. When I saw the profile angle of me excitedly smiling in response to bagging the huge whitetail, I noticed how my upper central incisors protruded so distinctly. Though it was likely that no one in the viewing audience cared what my teeth looked like, it didn't matter because I cared. I didn't like what I saw.

At that moment I decided that if I had to sell pop bottles and aluminum soda cans to get the cash required, I would get my teeth fixed.

It took a while to save up, but I finally managed to gather the funds. It wasn't cheap, but today I don't feel self-conscious about my profile when I smile. Even though my wallet took a big hit, I was able to change something I considered unacceptable.

If you never expect perfection from a
person, you'll never be disappointed.

Author unknown

On the "accept the unchangeable" side of the coin, my voice will never be as low as I'd like. When I hear country music artists like Don Williams and Alan Jackson singing with rich lower tones, I jokingly say, "Someday when I get out of puberty, I'll have a voice like that." It's a statement that contains a little levity, but I admit I'm serious about the desire.

While I would love to have the compelling quality that I believe a deeper voice could lend to my singing, I know it's not going to happen. Even with voice lessons that could possibly increase my range a little, I'll never possess the depth of sound I wish for my vocal renditions. For that reason I've chosen to accept the unchangeable.

One thing that helps me keep a positive attitude regarding my higher-pitched voice is that it blends well with that of my longtime, very talented singing partner, Annie. My wife has an alto voice in the range of popular country artist Anne Murray. Strangely enough, Annie's and my voices complement each other well. When I bring this unchangeable voice issue up to Annie, she always comforts me by saying, "Steve, if we both had lower voices we'd sound like two bumble bees in a barrel." She's right. So I've come to accept my voice as an asset to our musical performance.

Many years ago, my Grandfather Steele told me a story that helped me appreciate the peace-giving value of recognizing something acceptable in that which is unchangeable. He was a coal miner in West Virginia and had a fellow worker who, appropriately, was named Little Joe. I put his story in the following lyric.

Made for the Mines

Look inside that coal mine, way yonder in the back
You might see his eyes shining, white against the black
He's been there before the sun came up; he'll be there
    when it falls
We all call him Little Joe—he's only four-feet tall

He was made for the mines, made to work that coal
All day long way down in that hole
We all agreed that five-foot seam was a very cruel design
All except for Little Joe—he was made for the mines

If you're born in West Virginia, way back in the hills
If your daddy worked the coal mine, you know you
    probably will
Little Joe knew his fate, but he didn't seem to mind at all
'Cause when you're born a Shetland pony, any mine
    is plenty tall[6]

Now, O LORD, You are our Father, we are the clay, and You our potter; and all of us are the work of Your hand (Isaiah 64:8).

On the contrary, who are you, O man, who answers back to God? The thing molded will not say to the molder, "Why did you make me like this," will it? Or does not the potter have a right over the clay, to make from the same lump one vessel for honorable use and another for common use? (Romans 9:20-21).

"Never Brag Before the Battle"

Televised competitions, such as *American Idol, America's Got Talent, American Ninja Warrior,* as well as many athletic games that air often include interviews with the participants just before they compete. During these short features, I frequently see contestants give wide, confident smiles to the camera and say something akin too:

- "You're looking at the next 'American Idol'!"
- "I'm totally ready. I'm gonna win this whole thing."
- "I've been training for nine months for this moment, and I'm taking the trophy home today."
- "Nobody can stop us. Go blue (or green or yellow...)!"

These very assertive declarations are usually accompanied by finger-pointing and head nodding at the audience and camera lens, a raised arm pump, and maybe a primal yell of some sort. Then the show I'm watching transitions to the actual competition, be it singing, performing magic, doing acrobatics, attempting to get by some ridiculously difficult obstacles, playing a sport—football, baseball, basketball, snow skiing, boxing, wrestling—or a thousand other settings for challenging people's skills. And the drama begins.

I can't number how many times I've watched the braggarts fail to live up to their promises. As their faces show the agony of defeat, I can hear their unfulfilled claims reverberating in my mind. When that happens, I always think of the biblical warning found in the book of 1 Kings, chapter 20.

A king named Ben-hadad sent word to another king named Ahab that he was coming to take all his silver, gold, beautiful wives, and children.

King Ahab sent word back to Ben-hadad saying he wouldn't let that happen.

Then Ben-hadad sent Ahab a declaration of victory—even *before* his army left camp.

That's when Ahab sent a messenger to Ben-hadad. "Let not him who girds on his armor boast like him who takes it off" (verse 11).

In the end, King Ahab was the victor. For that reason, his advice to Ben-hadad is worthy of everyone's attention, including those who do battles on theater stages and in athletic stadiums, workplaces, classrooms, and other settings where competitions are found.

15

"Don't Mistake My Compassion for Stupidity"

I won't forget what happened the morning my dear wife woke up and headed to the kitchen to begin preparing breakfast for a group of young musicians we were lodging overnight. The only female in the band was a young lady who was a friend of a friend. Because we felt compassion for traveling groups, when she called and asked if she and her musical comrades could stay over at our house on their way through our town to their next gig, we were happy to accommodate them.

They were all unmarried, and their ages ranged from 19 to 22. To keep to biblical teachings and our moral standards, Annie had prepared beds upstairs for each of the boys and the girl was to use the pull-out couch bed that was downstairs in our sunroom.

On the evening they arrived, we fed them dinner. Afterward they piled back into in their van and headed out for an evening of touring the music venues in the city of Nashville. We were in bed asleep when they returned.

We assumed they would find their way to their respective sleeping spots when they came into the house. When morning came, we planned to go to their rooms to wake them up for a healthy, substantial breakfast. But that's not what happened.

Just before eight o'clock the next morning, I was still in our bedroom when I heard a raised voice coming from the sunroom. I could tell it was Annie speaking in her stern motherly voice—the one I'd heard her use when she was correcting our children as they grew up. I knew someone was getting a lecture. Later Annie told me about it.

When she walked into the kitchen, she could see into the sunroom and noticed that instead of a single body in the pull-out couch bed, there were three. She marched into the room and found two boys and a girl sprawled out and sawing logs. Thankfully they were all fully dressed.

In a tone of voice that immediately roused the trio of rule breakers, she said, "What gave you boys the idea that it would be permissible for you to sleep in the same bed as this girl? Did you mess with her? Did you touch her?"

The boys struggled to speak clearly through their half-wakened minds. They managed a nervous "No, ma'am!"

Then Annie's glaring eyes went to the young lady. "And what gave you the idea that we would allow you to have these boys in your bed in our house?"

The stunned young men sat up, threw their legs over the edge of the bed, grabbed their shoes, and headed upstairs.

The young woman showed very sincere regret that she'd abused Annie's good graces and hospitality. She assured my wife that no sexual touching had gone on in the bed.

Annie accepted her apology but not her explanation. The young musician said the boys were just too tired to make the climb upstairs to their rooms and, furthermore, they didn't want to wake us up. Nope, Annie didn't buy it.

After the band had breakfast and pulled away, Annie and I sat and had coffee together. We discussed what had happened, and I commended Annie for courageously confronting the youngsters. She thanked me and then quipped, "It's never a good thing to mistake my compassion for stupidity." I asked her to elaborate, and I totally agreed with what she said.

"My compassion for someone doesn't make me brain dead or dumb enough to be unaware of any attempt to deceive me. Instead, my compassion makes me more aware of that kind of treatment. Sure, I'll continue to show compassion to them, but I'll love them enough to let them know that I know when they're trying to pull the wool over my eyes."

I was quite impressed with Annie's savvy approach to showing kindness. I was hopeful that the three young band members got the message that it's not right to take advantage of someone's benevolence. If they did, not only will it serve them well as they travel on down the road of life, but the next kind-hearted host who opens their home to them will also benefit by it.

Young men and women: If you have dinner
with your date's parents and he or she insists
on helping cleanup afterward instead of sitting
with you on the couch, your date is a keeper!

Steve Chapman

16

"God Feeds the Birds, but He Doesn't Put Food in Their Nests"

In the early mornings I like to sit in our sunroom and watch the birds in our backyard. I'm amazed to see how industrious our winged guests are as they hop around in the grass looking and listening for bugs and worms they hope will become breakfast.

I don't know what it is about our backyard that makes it such a popular restaurant. Maybe it's the rich soil that makes it a good worm habitat. Or it's possible that our property is the only one in the area that hasn't been doused with chemicals that kill weeds and various kinds of crawling critters. For whatever reason, the gathering of many feathers is an enjoyable sight, and they're definitely welcome to have all the bugs they want.

One morning as I watched the birds foraging for food, I saw a picture of how God has chosen to feed mankind. All we need is in His backyard, but God doesn't drop food into our houses. Just as I don't go out and gather worms and bugs and deliver it to the birds' nests, we who are able-bodied are expected to go out and gather what God provides.

Unfortunately, today there are plenty of healthy "birds" who sit and wait for someone to bring them some worms. They're called *takers*. Some of them have been trained by over-giving parents to have a taker attitude. Others have been conditioned by an over-reaching government to sit dependently in their nests and wait for handouts.

Granted, there are plenty of legitimate receivers who, for various reasons, can't get to the backyard of the workplace and gather their portion of daily "grubs," but the takers, those who can but won't go do their own gathering, are a burden on society. When my early morning viewing of the industrious birds is interrupted by fear that the takers in our nation are outnumbering the givers, I know what to do to restore some hope. I can leave the sunroom and go to our front door. About a hundred yards from our front steps is a county highway. Even though it's considered a country road, between the morning hours of six and eight, it's filled with cars, vans, big trucks, and buses carrying people who are going to the "backyards" of their employment. Some are headed to the nearby water-heater plant where they work, and some are driving to offices in Nashville, 30 miles down the road. Many in our area are off to their jobs in the town of Clarksville, which boasts a university and, nearby, a large military installation. The work traffic is a heartwarming sight to behold, and it's an uplifting realization that there are still folks who believe that God provides our food, but He doesn't bring it to our houses. He wants us to work! The apostle Paul wrote:

> Even when we were with you, we used to give you this order: if anyone is not willing to work, then he is not to eat, either (2 Thessalonians 3:10).

My philosophy is that "takers may eat better, but givers sleep better."

17

"Givedends"

*When you donate to a cause that is dear to God's heart,
you will always reap great givedends.*

When people invest in a company's work, the company makes sure their shareholders experience a gain called a "dividend." The yield usually comes in the form of money. In a similar way, when people invest in God's work, He sees to it that His "heirholders" get a return I like to call a "givedend." This divine version of economics is explained in 2 Corinthians 9:6-9:

> He who sows sparingly will also reap sparingly, and he who sows bountifully will also reap bountifully. Each one must do just as he has purposed in his heart, not grudgingly or under compulsion, for God loves a cheerful giver. And God is able to make all grace abound to you, so that always having all sufficiency in everything, you may have an abundance for every good deed; as it is written, "He scattered abroad, He gave to the poor, His righteousness endures forever."

While *getting* should never be the motivation for *giving*, it is always inspiring to hear stories that illustrate how sowing abundantly can result in reaping a bountiful crop of givedends. One example is found in John 6. It's the familiar account of the young lad who gave his entire lunch of 2 fish and 5 barley loaves to Jesus and His disciples. The Lord used the boy's offering to miraculously feed a hungry crowd of more than 5000!

Afterward there were 12 baskets of barley-loaf fragments left over. Though the passage doesn't state it, I'm convinced the boy took a good portion of the yield back home with him. No doubt he got a firsthand taste of what real givedends are all about.

The bread and fish story isn't only a great illustration of the benefits of giving, but it's also an excellent example of the fact that givers don't always have to give money. In fact, there are many other things that, if given liberally, will yield a plentiful return. One of them is forgiveness. Luke 6:36-38 NIV says:

> Be merciful, just as your Father is merciful...Forgive, and you will be forgiven. Give, and it will be given to you. A good measure, pressed down, shaken together and running over, will be poured into your lap. For with the measure you use, it will be measured to you.

How gracious of God to be so generous to those who give. He proves over and over again that His givedends are endless.

18

"God Is the Maker, Man Is the Mixer"

Man has never made anything. He only takes what God
has already made and rearranges it.

While standing in line waiting for the doors to open at a concert venue, I struck up a conversation with the guy behind me. We'd never met, and during our chat I learned that his work was in the field of commercial construction design. I was awed by his description of what it took for his company to build one of the tallest and most impressive buildings in downtown Nashville. The edifice's official name is "The AT&T Building," but because of its unique shape at the top, the locals call it "the Batman Building."

He smiled when I told him that I considered his work in construction one of the most admirable and amazing things a person can do. To be involved in the making of something like a house, a high-rise, a bridge, a cruise ship, and many other structures mankind builds is, in my opinion, a career that deserves the utmost respect. But something happened the next morning that altered my thinking about humans making things.

I went for my "beauty walk," which is what Annie calls the four-mile round-trip trek I do for exercise. I was listening to the New International Version of the Book of John on my smartphone. I started with chapter 1, and after just three verses I had to stop the app because something captured my attention. Here's what I heard:

> In the beginning was the Word, and the Word was with
> God, and the Word was God. He was with God in the
> beginning. Through Him all things were made; without
> Him nothing was made that has been made.

After hearing those words, it occurred to me that according to John's writing, mankind has made nothing. Instead, the Word of God says, "through [Christ] all things were made." I pondered the far-reaching scope of those words for about a tenth of a mile. As I walked along, I looked down at the pavement. And that's when another thought came that was so astounding I had to say it aloud:

> Mankind didn't make the concrete under my feet. He only
> took the ingredients God had already made and rearranged
> them. Without God's gift of intelligence to mankind that
> is required to figure out how to rearrange His created ele-
> ments, I'd be walking on a dirt road.

Then my thoughts went to the fellow I'd met the evening before and to the massive building we'd talked about. I realized that neither he nor any other of his coworkers had ever actually made anything. They took the things that already existed and reorganized them into useful structures.

The next time you walk on a sidewalk or stand next to a skyscraper, stop and take a really close look at the concrete. You'll see that it's a mixture of sand (made by God), gravel (made by God), a bonding agent called Portland cement (a concoction of calcium, silicon, aluminum, iron, and other ingredients made by God), and water (made by the hands of God).

The bottom line? God is the maker, man is the mixer! Even the brain mankind uses to come up with new mixtures is something God made.

19

"Everything Said Should Be True, but Not Everything True Should Be Said"

I traveled to the town of Deville, Louisiana, for an early fall event called "Blessing of the Hunt," held at Longview Baptist Church. My return flight to Tennessee didn't depart until Sunday afternoon, which allowed me the opportunity to go to church that morning with my hosts. I had no idea that it would be the day I would sit in the most enjoyable and informative Sunday school class I've ever attended. It was called "The Camo Class."

By nine thirty, the room was filled with some of the most delightful men on the globe. There were some hilarious exchanges between the guys as they gathered. I could tell they were all the best of friends.

The subject of the lesson was "communication," and the featured scriptural passage was Ephesians 4:25-31. The opening verse of this passage says, "Laying aside falsehood, SPEAK TRUTH EACH ONE of you WITH HIS NEIGHBOR..." (Ephesians 4:25). As the men discussed the need to be truthful whenever they speak, I heard some honest confessions about how difficult it was to follow the admonition in Scripture.

Of all that was said about the verse, one particular statement especially caught my ear. With a classic Southern drawl, one of the gentlemen said, "When I was growin' up, my daddy always told me, 'Son, everything that's said should be true, but not everything that's true should be said.'" He followed with an example of how his dad's sage advice could present a dangerous risk. "What if my wife comes downstairs one evening after getting ready to go out and says to me, 'Do I look fat in these pants?' What's a man supposed to do when that happens?"

The room immediately erupted in laughter. It was strong and boisterous at first, but then I noticed it pretty quickly turned into nervous chuckles. It was as though the gravity of the example given began to fall on each husband. For a moment we all just stared at each other in wide-eyed, scared silence. Not one of us could offer a marriage-saving answer.

The class continued for another 20 minutes, with other aspects of communication being discussed, and then dismissal time came. I had a feeling that as every man exited the room, he was still wondering what he was supposed to say if his wife asked *that* question. I suspect that every one of us knew that the only hope we had was that we'd never hear it. We left prayerfully.

I've never been hurt by what I didn't say.

U.S. President Calvin Coolidge

20

"The 200 for 100 Rule"

By the time our son, Nathan, was in his final year of homeschooling, his musical skills were quite advanced. Also, his understanding of "signal path" (a term used in the world of audio engineering) was exceeded only by his passion for it. It was for these reasons I decided that his senior class project would be the challenge of planning, producing, performing, and directing a live music video.

The details that had to be covered seemed endless, but Nathan appeared to enjoy the process. I helped only with hiring the sound and video crew and doing the advertising. He did all the rest of the work, which included gathering the musicians, finding the venue for doing the taping, arranging the rehearsals, writing the song charts for each player, and completing a list of other details too long to go into.

I was quite impressed with how Nathan handled all the responsibility that was given to him. I could see that the challenge was occupying his mind nearly 24/7. But one of the main things I noticed most was how much practice Nathan managed to include among all the other things he had to do. If I had a dollar for every hour he was in his room or in our studio basement running through the songs that were on his set list, I would've probably had the cash to cover the expense of the four extra musicians, the performance hall, the audio and video techs, the printing of the advertisements. and all the other facets needed for the recording. I finally asked him if the reason he was practicing so much was because he was so nervous about the concert. His answer has haunted me (in a good way) since that day.

He said, "Of course, I'm nervous about playing with a band and doing it live to tape, but the way I figure it, if I'm going to get somewhere near 100 percent on stage, I have to practice 200 percent."

You can count the seeds in an apple, but
you can't count the apples in a seed.

Author unknown

The production and filming went extremely well. As for Nathan's performance, parentally speaking, on a scale of 1 to 10 it was a strong 11! It was obvious that his self-imposed practice policy had paid off. I was inspired to apply the same wisdom to my work as a performer. To this day, when I'm scheduled to sing and speak to an audience, the concept of 200 for 100 always comes to me as I prepare.

I believe this is a great policy and worthy of passing on to you. Whether you perform on a stage, teach in a classroom, play a sport on a church league, or anything else that requires preparation, keep in mind the 200 for 100 rule. It will work for you.

A slack hand causes poverty, but the hand of the diligent makes rich (Proverbs 10:4 ESV).

21

"People Are like Flowers, and Some Are Better Suited to Shade"

When Annie and I got the shocking news about the moral failure of a well-known Christian celebrity, we offered up a prayer on the person's behalf. We did so because not only did we know him personally, but we also knew that his world, including his family's world, would be rocked by the invading and merciless media. As we discussed the situation and the damaging fallout that would result from his unwise choices, Annie made a statement about the person that had its roots in her experience as a gardener. She said, "Some flowers don't do well in direct, full sunlight. Some do better in the shade, like impatiens or pansies. It seems that our friend is not like a Gerbera daisy that can take the full impact of the sun."

Annie went on to explain. "Our friend is very talented and easy on the eyes, but because those around him see that they have a chance to make some cash by pushing him onto the public stage, they chose to ignore his weaknesses. His frail personal traits and character flaws did not make him a good candidate for the heat of the public eye and the temptations that come with it. He'd do a lot better in the soft shade of the backstage of life."

Don't envy the person who has
great wealth because you don't know
what it cost them to get it.

Author unknown

I was astounded by the wisdom in Annie's very astute observation. I thought of other disgraced public figures, both secular and religious, whose stories might have turned out differently had they not been placed in the spotlight of fame. Instead of being scorched by the self-inflating rays of too much attention, they might have served more effectively with their skills in a less-exposed setting.

Annie added one more thing to her gardening illustration that I seriously took to heart and can recommend to you as well. She said, "When I'm tempted to add the harsh glare of my judgment to their sad situation, I must keep in mind that if I were to be placed under the same spotlight, I too might wilt in the heat."

── 22 ──

"The Less You See,
the More You Hear"

Annie and I have been asked on several occasions why we never have a band to back us up on stage when we sing together. We are very aware that our answer to the question reveals an odd mindset, but we firmly believe it holds some wisdom worth incorporating into our performances: "The less you see, the more you hear."

In our thinking, the most important components of our presentations are the messages in our song lyrics and teachings. The words are meant to instruct as well as encourage and entertain various family members. Our concern that our listeners will enjoy the harmony that comes with living peacefully together within a family is great enough that we will do what we can to keep that message our primary feature. We want husbands, wives, children, grandkids, grandparents, singles, singles again, and engaged couples to hear what we're saying in our songs. In order to help our audience focus on what is said, our stage will not have a lot of moving parts for their eyes to get distracted by.

We base our preference for a "calm" stage on our personal experience with concert going. One particular event we attended that especially reinforced our policy of limiting the movement around our microphones took place in our hometown of Nashville. We won some tickets to the event from a radio station, and we looked forward to cashing in on some free entertainment.

The show opened with a couple of solo songwriters who took their turns telling some great stories in their songs. We found ourselves completely engaged in their memorable lyrics that were supported by their well-done guitar playing. When they finished, the next act filed on stage. There were a total of nine musicians, and what happened for the next 20 minutes is forever etched in our minds.

If you're the most important person in your
circle of friends, you need a bigger circle.

Annie Chapman

From one end of the stage to the other, we saw a banjo, a washboard, a fiddle, a snare drum, an accordion, two guitars, a mandolin, and an upright bass. From the downbeat of the first of six very up-tempo songs to the last note of the closing tune, each player strummed, pounded, plucked, and squeezed their instruments so quickly that their hands were almost a blur. In addition, they all jumped up and down the entire time they played and sang. We broke out in a sweat just watching them.

On the drive home, Annie and I talked about how little we remembered about the nine-member group other than their lightning-fast fingers and the rhythmic pogo stick jumping they did. Together we couldn't come up with a full line from any of their songs. We agreed that even though it might be more entertaining for an audience and for us as performers to have a stage full of musicians, our goal of featuring our message would still be best served by erring on the side of "the less you see, the more you hear."

23

"Having a Good Reason Doesn't Mean It Should Be Done"

Years ago I heard a story about an evangelist who was holding a seven-night revival. Each evening when he began preaching, a man about five pews back in an aisle seat would heckle him. For three nights the evangelist endured the annoying interruptions coming from the man who always sat in the same place. On the fourth night, when the heckler threw another verbal barb, the evangelist decided he'd had enough.

As he continued preaching, he walked out from behind the pulpit and headed down the aisle. When he reached the pew where the man was sitting, the audience member said, "Boring! Get on with it!" At that the frustrated preacher made a tight fist with his right hand and used it to sock the heckler firmly on his jaw.

Immediately the pastor, an elder, and a couple of deacons swept in to deal with the chaos that erupted. Bewildered by the visiting preacher's method of silencing the protester, the pastor asked, "Brother, why didn't you ask God to take care of this matter for you?"

The evangelist's response? "Why would I ask God to do something I can do?"

While this story isn't true (at least I hope it's not), there is a good lesson to be learned from it. The evangelist may have had a good reason to pummel the heckler, but it wasn't a good enough reason to actually do it.

This bit of wisdom is worth keeping in mind for a lot of situations other than reacting to someone who is sparking your anger. For example, being tired of feeling lonely might be a good reason for a person to pursue getting married, but it isn't a good reason to say yes to someone who is overly jealous, dangerously possessive, or abusive.

Another example worth mentioning is the person who dives into the social media pool because he or she feels a need to be liked. That may be a good reason to get involved, but in my opinion it's not enough to justify exposing so much private information to the entire world.

Finally, I have my own example to offer for why having a good reason to do something doesn't mean it should be done. It may not be as impacting as the previous examples, but it made on impression on me. When Annie and I were first married, we drove a 1950 Chevy we named Sarah (because she was old and still productive, just like Sarah in the Bible). Needing to keep our house warm in the winter with our freestanding Franklin fireplace, we traded our Sarah for a load of firewood during our second year of marriage. Because I had a special affection for Sarah, I sure did hate to see her leave with the man who delivered the wood.

Forty is the old age of youth
and the youth of old age.

Victor Borge
(paraphrased)

About 20 years later, I was driving on a back road in our county and went by a house with a very nicely restored 1950 Chevy sitting in the front yard. The "for sale" sign in the window caught my eye, and I hit the brakes, turned around, and pulled into the driveway of the home.

I was grateful to see a man in the garage behind the house. When he came toward my truck, I got out to greet him. I asked him about the price he was asking for his antique Chevy. When he told me a figure that was just short of $9000, I started mentally adjusting our family budget. I thanked him for the info, got his phone number, and climbed back into my pickup. On my way home, I dreamed about owning the vintage vehicle.

I had a very good reason, I thought, to go to the bank and dip into our savings to get the old-but-beautiful car. The idea of Annie and me driving around sitting side-by-side in a vehicle that was nearly a twin sister of the one we'd used while dating and in our first married years seemed like one of the most romantic things a husband could do. It was very enticing to go for the "Best Hubby in the World Award." But I was also well aware that we didn't have the extra cash required to get the antique symbol of our enduring love.

It wasn't easy, but to avoid putting an unnecessary strain on our finances I made the hard decision to let the old Chevy go. Though I didn't get to go buy "Sarah 2" and take her home for my dear wife, I'm grateful that I took to heart the adage that "having a good reason doesn't mean it should be done."

24

"One Man's Junk Is Another Man's Junk"

If we're home on a Saturday from spring to late fall, and I wake early in the morning to find that my dear wife isn't at my side, I don't worry. I know that more than likely she's gotten up and gone "saling." She openly admits that the enjoyment of cruising from one neighborhood "pond" to another to check out the yard sales is sort of like an addictive drug. She also admits that she has no plans to break the habit.

Annie normally doesn't ask me if I want to go along on her weekend adventures because she knows I'm not a fan of going to garage sales. One of the reasons is that I've come to the conclusion that the well-known saying "One man's junk is another man's treasure" is simply not true. I came to grips with this rarely recognized fact on the day we held our own yard sale.

It took us nearly 50 trips from our garage, attic, and storage building to our driveway to carry all the stuff we decided to sell. The "department store" that was spread across the concrete and into our grass included an array of items such as plastic toys, various brands and sizes of suitcases, a plethora of dishes and kitchen utensils, picture frames, clothes, rugs, and even an unused kerosene heater.

When we finally completed the huge display and finished pricing each item, I stood back and studied the collection. That's when I realized that most of the things we were selling came from other garage sales. Much of what we (and I use "we" only because Annie and I are one through marriage) thought was a treasure when it was purchased with our hard-earned quarters and dollars wasn't a treasure at all. Yes, maybe at the moment the item seemed valuable and possibly even needed, but eventually it ended up in the heap of junk that was now covering our driveway.

That was the day I gathered up the nerve to say something out loud for my beloved to hear. I pulled my shoulders back in preparation for defending my stance and said with a voice that was as loving as I could make it sound, "Well, here's proof that one man's junk is another man's junk."

Annie shot me a stare with her beautiful hazel eyes that told me I was treading on sacred ground. When she put her hands on her hips, I knew she'd just loaded her word cannon with some powerful ammo. I stood ready to receive the salvo.

When she spoke, I was completely surprised.

"You're right, sweetheart. This is ridiculous. We have to get rid of this stuff, and we should never go to another yard sale again."

And "we" didn't—for two Saturdays.

25

"A Heart Will Never Be Right Until It's Right at Home"

Have you ever gotten in a tiff with your spouse, child, or other family member just before leaving for work, school, or another destination? If so, did you notice that nothing or no place beyond the walls of your home seemed happy or peaceful? The reason for this is that the turmoil that arose between your family member and you didn't stay behind. Instead, it went with you.

On the other hand, if you spent the morning getting ready to head out and all the while there's goodwill between your loved ones and you, did you notice how the rest of the world seemed like a happy place when you were out there in it?

The good news is that if you leave your house in an uproar and your churning soul is making the rest of the world a not so great place to be, there's always the option of either turning around and going back or making a phone call to make things right. With just a quick return to the house or a two-minute phone call, along with an attitude of humility, whatever has gotten bent can usually be straightened.

> If you started your marriage with nothing
> and you've managed to keep most of it,
> you're probably happier than you realize.
>
> **Steve and Annie Chapman**

I can personally testify to how making things right at home can make the rest of the world seem right. Just before I walked out the door one morning to go to a meeting, Annie was getting off the phone with a friend. My wife told me that she'd just accepted an invitation for both of us to go to dinner that evening with the couple. That idea was nowhere near what I had planned for the evening. I'd had my sights set on being in a deer stand. So my reaction to the news about dinner was less than nice. The red on my face and the tone in my voice as I protested the plans left no doubt in Annie's mind that I wasn't happy.

Annie picked up the phone and started dialing her friend to cancel the date. As I closed the door behind me, I mumbled, "Don't call her. I'll go."

I pulled out of the driveway with a little steam still coming from my collar. Before I was out of sight of our house, I was dealing with a grinding in my gut about having left Annie in such a huff. She didn't deserve the brunt of my ire. Not wanting to be late for the meeting and not wanting to go to it with a feeling of unease in my spirit, I pushed the speed dial button on my cell phone that would connect me with home.

Annie answered with a tentative sound in her voice. She listened quietly as I admitted what a jerk I'd been with my response to the plans she'd made. She could have just agreed, but she nicely added her forgiveness. The best part of the conversation was how good I felt after we finished. The world was right again because things were right at home.

> Let all bitterness and wrath and anger and clamor and slander be put away from you, along with all malice. Be kind to one another, tender-hearted, forgiving each other, just as God in Christ also has forgiven you (Ephesians 4:31-32).

26

"Play or Not, Your Chances of Winning Are the Same"

I was third in line at the convenience store checkout counter where I'd stopped to get some gas and a snack. The customer in front of me looked a bit disheveled in clothes that obviously hadn't been washed for a while. Though I was aware that I can't always judge a book by its cover, I surmised from his appearance that he was a man of limited resources.

If my speculation was correct it made it even more difficult to understand what happened when he was invited to take his turn at the counter. He handed the cashier a $20 bill and said, "I'll take two 'Power 7s.'"

The items I watched him buy were two $10 lottery tickets. Their worth was up to $250,000 each if they were winners. As the lady opened the clear plastic container that held the paper dreams and ripped two colorful tickets off the roll, I fought the urge to say what I was thinking. I didn't win the fight.

I knew it was none of my business to offer the man my observation, but I figured if no one else was going to appeal to his better judgment it might as well be me. So to a total stranger I said as calmly and nicely as I could, "Excuse me, sir. You do realize, don't you, that your chances of winning are the same whether you buy a ticket or not?" After the entire sentence was out of my mouth, I noticed that everyone in the vicinity of the checkout counter stopped talking and moving. It was as though someone had pushed the cosmic pause and mute buttons. The two people behind me, the cashier, and the man who stood there with two unscratched tickets stared at me for what felt like a full hour. Probably two or three seconds passed before the world started moving again. The man just rolled his eyes and grunted as he walked away and headed toward the exit. At least he didn't hit me.

I left with my bottle of cold tea and package of crackers, climbed into my truck, and drove away. Though it was an awkward moment for us both, I felt good about having sowed the seeds of common sense in the mind of the stranger. I imagined him leaving the store and suddenly having a revelation about the fruitlessness of investing cash in the lottery. I fantasized that in response to what I'd said he would choose to use his funds in the future to buy things of greater value, such as groceries, fuel, shoes for his kids, and other such necessities in life. I could only hope that's what happened. I'll never know.

As I headed down the road, I thought of how many folks in our state and nation could benefit by avoiding the lottery trap. As a way of telling others what I told the man that day, I decided to put the advice in a song lyric. Here are the words that came to me after leaving the convenience store.

Play or Not

He's got bills comin' due
He sends the IRS his IOUs
He's got twenty-one years on a ten-year roof
But he gets in that line

He needs parts for his '68 Bel Air
Right now it's up on blocks just sittin' there
There are holes in his daughter's shoes, she needs a pair
But it's his time, he's next in line

They'll put another power ticket in the hands of the weak
And the ones who sell the dream call it a game

But they won't tell him the truth, if he plays or if he don't
The chances he will win are still the same
Play or not, his chances are the same

He dreams of what will happen on that day
When the numbers drop, and they fall his way
But if he had every dollar he's already paid
He could buy those shoes, pay some IOUs

And he could bring that old Bel Air back from the dead
The rain would be something not to dread
But there's a hunger for the game that must be fed
It's what a fool would choose
You gotta play to lose

They'll put another power ticket in the hands of the weak
And the ones who profit most call it a game
But they won't tell him the truth, if he plays or if he don't
The chances he will win are still the same
Play or not, his chances are the same[7]

———— ✦ ————

The love of money is a root of all sorts of evils, and some
by longing for it have wandered away from the faith and
pierced themselves with many griefs (1 Timothy 6:10).

27

"If Church Is Comfortable, You Might Need to Move Along"

Annie and I have never forgotten what a pastor said at the beginning of a Sunday morning worship service several years ago. Along with the other attendees, we stood in the sanctuary and visited with our friends prior to the top of the hour that the service was scheduled to begin. When the music started all of us suspended our visiting and settled into the pews.

After we sang a verse and chorus of a familiar hymn, the music minister didn't lead us in another song. Instead, he deliberately let the room grow very quiet, as if he'd been instructed to do so. At that point, the pastor unhurriedly walked to the pulpit with his arms partly crossed and one hand on his chin. He stood at the podium for several seconds and pensively looked over the congregation before he spoke. We could tell by his expression that something of significance was on his heart.

"Saints," he started lovingly, "did you come here this morning hoping you'd encounter something that would help you leave here a different person? The question I have on my heart is, if you didn't come here this morning to be changed, why did you bother coming?"

He paused for a moment to let us process what he'd said.

"For the past few Sundays I've wanted to ask you the question you just heard. I know it sounds rather probing, but just know that it won't be the last time I'll ask it. As often as I can, I want to remind you that according to Philippians 1:6, God, who began a good work in you, will be faithful to complete it. If you embrace that promise, then just like a child who changes as he or she gets older, we should expect to change as we mature in Christ. I long to see some of that change happen—or at least get started—right here in this building."

The pastor had our attention with his heartfelt words. What he was saying rang true in our hearts. What he said next put a huge exclamation point on his statements.

"Here's the deal, saints. If you're coming to this church because you feel comfortable here, then you're not going to the right church. The truth of the matter is, if that's the case, then I'm not doing my job right."

I wanted to stand and applaud the pastor for offering such a bold challenge from the pulpit, but I thought it best to let the challenge chips fall where they may. His words certainly cut into my idea of what it traditionally means to "go to church." Annie had the same reaction.

Since that day, our family has moved a couple of times. Each time as we've considered what church to attend, we've recalled that pastor's words. We agreed that if we wanted to grow in our faith, then feeling comfortable would not be one of the criteria we'd use for choosing a church home. Instead, we decided to go where the truth is boldly preached so the fires of change are often lit under us. Without those flames, we know we'd eventually become complacent and possibly lukewarm in our faith—something God doesn't care for at all (Revelation 3:15-16).

Woe to those who are at ease in Zion (Amos 6:1).

28

"There Is No Grace for Borrowed Sorrow"

Many years ago, Annie and I attended a weekend seminar called Institute in Basic Youth Conflicts that was taught by a gentleman named Bill Gothard. During one of the sessions, he spoke about the blessing of God's boundless grace. It was encouraging to hear him expound on the statement the Lord said to Paul: "My grace is sufficient for you" (2 Corinthians 12:9).

As Dr. Gothard comforted us with the truth that God's grace extends even to our deepest sorrows and that He "knows our needs before we even ask," something happened that we won't forget. Gothard suddenly paused long enough to alert the massive crowd that he was about to say something we'd probably want to write down in our syllabus. Then he continued. I can't remember exactly how he worded it, but what I wrote was, "There is no grace for borrowed sorrow."

His explanation of the warning helped us understand that when something happens that causes an emotion like fear to grip us, we must remember that we can trust that God's grace will be applied. However, when we allow our minds to run irrationally toward all the other things that could have happened but didn't, essentially we step out from underneath the protective umbrella of God's grace.

One incident I recall that that illustrates "borrowed sorrow" took place in early 1968 in my hometown in West Virginia that sat along the Ohio River. My sister went out on a date with a boy, and they went across the river to eat at a restaurant. Because of the tragic fall of the Silver Bridge in December 1967, there was no way for traffic to cross the river other than by ferry. After leaving the restaurant and then going bowling, they headed back to our house around ten o'clock. The young man drove his car onto the boat and about halfway across the river the ferry's engine shut down.

With all the power gone, the lights went black and the radio was inoperative. Since it was pre-cell phone days and there was no emergency power source onboard, the crew had no way of communicating their need for a tow. They simply drifted down the river in total darkness.

When midnight came and there was no sign of my sister, we knew something was very wrong. It wasn't at all like her to be out so late. When 12:30 came, our family started coming unglued with worry. Still feeling the devastating effects of the sorrow that the bridge fall had caused, it's possible that we might have been a little more on edge than normal, but for whatever reason, our collective imaginations ran rampant.

Words like "kidnapped," "drowned," "eloped," and "rape" were tossed around. Tears flowed, anger levels rose, and restless pacing started. Then the phone rang.

Thankfully, a towboat that was pushing a barge upriver passed the drifting ferry and, with help from the towboat crew, word got to shore of their dilemma. Using the onboard radio and a list of phone numbers provided by the passengers, the towboat captain instructed his company to call the passengers' loved ones to let them know what had happened. We were very relieved to hear that my sister wasn't harmed and would be home soon.

Whenever I remember that troublesome night all those years ago, I wish someone would have walked into our living room and said, "Hey! Stop this madness. Rein in your wild horses of imagination. There is no grace for borrowed sorrow." How much more composed and courageous we might have been.

I've had plenty of opportunities to remember and apply Dr. Gothard's life-changing insight since that seminar. There have been issues, such as a suspicious lump under the skin, an intimidating letter from the IRS, an airplane engine that failed, and some dreadfully troublesome phone calls that have tempted me to mount the untamed stallion called Imagination. I wish I could say that I never did get on that wild horse and ride, but it wouldn't be true. There have been times when I've made the mistake of letting my thoughts run away with me. But thanks be to God! Though He offers no grace for borrowed sorrow, He does offer grace to the borrower.

> When my anxious thoughts multiply within me, Your consolations delight my soul (Psalm 94:19).

29

"The Pews Aren't Sitting in Church; the Church Is Sitting in Pews"

A deacon greeted a new visitor one Sunday morning in the lobby of the church and noticed that he was wearing a pair of well-worn blue jeans and tennis shoes. Because of the deacon's personal dislike of people attending church dressed so casually, when he shook the young man's hand he pulled him close and said in a half-whisper, "We don't allow jeans in the sanctuary. This is the house of God, and that kind of outfit is offensive to Him."

The deacon paused for just a moment to let the young fellow process his statement. Before he could say another word, the young man turned on his heels and headed out the door.

Standing nearby was a member of the church who overheard what the deacon had said to the visitor. After the service ended he went to the pastor and reported what had happened in the lobby. Troubled by the news, the pastor called the deacon into his office to discuss the matter.

"I hear that you had some concern about the attire of a young guest you met in the lobby this morning."

The deacon sounded defensive as he answered, "I did, indeed. He was dressed in a way that disrespects the house of God, in my opinion, and I informed him about it. I was going to invite him on in anyway, but before I could do it he left."

The pastor stood up. "Well, I'll take care of this. Next Sunday I'll let the entire congregation know what our stance is in regard to how people should dress when they come to church."

Feeling relieved that his pastor hadn't asked for the meeting to scold him for what he'd said to the first-time guest, the deacon smiled and said, "I'm glad you'll do it, pastor. I'll stand behind you on this issue."

The next Sunday came and the pastor deliberately waited until after the worship music was well underway before he entered the sanctuary. When he walked through the side door and onto the stage there was a momentary drop in volume in the singing as the congregation gave a somewhat melodic gasp. The sight they beheld stunned everyone in the room, especially the deacon who had made his clothing preference known to the young guest previously.

A man who wears a toupee to church should
never criticize a man who walks in wearing a hat.

Annie Chapman

The pastor was dressed in the jeans he wore to mow his yard and do other chores around his house, a tattered T-shirt with his college team logo on the front, and the tennis shoes he used for running. The pastor took his place in his big chair. When the singing ended and the folks sat down, there was a soft-but-distinct sound of whispering in the sanctuary. It was the pastor's turn to speak.

"Good morning, saints. I know you're shocked to see me dressed down this morning, but I wore these clothes to make a point. It came to my attention that there is some concern about the wearing of jeans in our sanctuary. Some folks sincerely believe they should never be worn in here."

By then there was dead silence in the building except for the pastor's voice.

"Folks, I agree that we should come to this building dressed as nicely as possible. It's a way of saying that we recognize God deserves our best. But the truth is, though this structure is a wonderful work of all your hands, it *is not* the place where God dwells." The pastor discreetly looked toward the deacon as he continued. "God has chosen to dwell in temples of clay. If you have repented of your sins and believed and accepted what Jesus did for you at the cruel cross, and if you have received the resurrected life that is offered with His redeeming grace, then God's spirit dwells *within you.* That makes *you* the church, not this building. This is simply where God's temples of clay gather for corporate worship."

The pastor was grateful to see some agreeable nodding of heads as he closed his remarks.

"I'm sure all of us are excited when seekers show up at the door of this church building. We're excited because we believe we can point them to the only source of real and lasting peace. That's why we built this marvelous place. But keep this in mind: It's not how their bodies are dressed when they get here that's important. It's how their souls are dressed when they leave. If they hear the gospel of Jesus and respond to it, Romans 13:14 teaches that they "put on the Lord Jesus Christ," which means they leave clothed in His righteousness. And in due time, perhaps they'll want to come dressed physically in a way that testifies to what has happened spiritually. But even if they don't, they'll be welcome here because if God accepts them we will too."

From that day on there was never another reported confrontation between the rule-keeping deacon and visitors regarding their clothing. The pastor had successfully taught him, as well as the rest of the congregation, that the pews aren't sitting in the church; the church is sitting in the pews.

> I write so that you will know how one ought to conduct himself in the household of God, which is the church of the living God, the pillar and support of the truth (1 Timothy 3:15).

"Greatness Isn't Found in Perfection; It's Found in Recovery"

Several years ago Annie and I received an invitation to sing at the celebration of the twenty-fifth anniversary of the radio broadcast ministry of Focus on the Family. We were asked to sing the song we'd written called *Turn Your Heart Toward Home*. That song was used in their film series by the same title.

The audience for the event would be filled with state and national government dignitaries, as well as a host of notable individuals from the Christian community. Because such an impressive gathering would be there, we tried to approach the event with as much calm as we could muster. However, by the time the day came for the celebration, we were puddles of nerves.

After rehearsing the song with our prerecorded music track at sound check, we were sitting in the green room immersed in stage fright. Suddenly I got an idea that I thought might make our performance a little less demanding and less stressful. I went to the soundman and told him to eliminate the track for our song. We were going to do a simple guitar and duet rendition. The format for the song would be one verse, the chorus, and then the addition of a verse and chorus of the old familiar song "Softly and Tenderly." Instead of a full four minutes of performance, our abbreviated medley would reduce our time on stage to a manageable two-and-a-half minutes.

At last we were introduced. I started finger-picking the song "Turn

Your Heart Toward Home" on my guitar. All was going well until I finished my verse and chorus. Annie was supposed to begin singing the original version of "Softly and Tenderly," but instead, much to her surprise and mine, she began singing the words to that melody that was made famous by Cynthia Clawson and was used in the classic movie *Trip to Bountiful.*

I didn't know any of the chords to the movie version and had to hunt for them as Annie sang. I could only guess what the progression was in the verse and, thankfully, my guessing worked. The chorus, however, was much more complicated, and that was when I was sure our performance would become a complete train wreck. I glanced over at Annie as she sang, and I could see the expression on her face. It was what I imagine a NASCAR driver's face looks like just before he or she hits the wall at 200 miles or so per hour.

Sweat was beginning to run down the back of my legs, and the intense nervousness I felt made my fingers feel like they'd died and been petrified. I couldn't believe what was about to go down in the annals of our musical history. But when the verse ended, something wonderfully surprising happened that I'm convinced was divine intervention. Neither of us is sure how but by a miracle of God, when Annie started into the *chorus* of "Softly and Tenderly," she reverted to the original version. I knew the chords, and as I played along I quietly breathed a huge sigh of relief that seemed to last a whole minute.

We harmonized the last words of the medley, I strummed a final chord on my guitar, and I walked off the stage behind Annie. I honestly can't remember if there was applause or a collective sympathetic moan from the audience as we headed back to our dinner table. My brain was mush from the strain I'd just experienced. We didn't sit down in our designated chairs; instead, we collapsed into them.

The need is not always the call.

Bob Hughey

Across the table was a gentleman I didn't know. I spent a minute or two recovering from what I assumed was an utter musical disaster before I finally introduced myself to our tablemate. I learned that he was also a singer and was scheduled to perform later in the evening. Assuming he would find our fresh and frightening story to be interesting, I told him what had just happened to us on stage.

After I finished he said, "Steve, Annie, I didn't hear what you just described. Your medley was seamless and beautiful."

We looked at each other in shock. When we looked back at our new best friend, we said, "Are you serious? It sounded okay?"

That's when he said the words we will never forget for as long as we have memory: "Greatness isn't found in perfection; it's found in recovery!"

Oh, what comfort those words were to us that night. And they have been a source of consolation to our souls several times since, when we've had a "near stage death" experience caused by forgotten lyrics or misplaced chords. Maybe they'll be of help to you too.

> A righteous man falls seven times, and rises again, but the wicked stumble in time of calamity (Proverbs 24:16).

31

"Life Is Rigged; We Can't Do It Right Without God"

I must credit my Louisiana friend Ken Fletcher for this bit of wisdom. I heard him say it in his message to his daughter and her groom during their wedding ceremony. He tenderly offered a lot of important insights to the young couple as he spoke, but when he told them that they could not "do marriage right" without God's help, a smile came to my face.

I knew if the lovely bride and her chosen beloved would embrace such a profound truth and lean on the Lord to help them be good mates to one another, then they would experience an enjoyable life together. I prayed silently during the wedding that they would not try to do their relationship on their own because it simply doesn't work. There are plenty of aspects of marriage to use as examples of this fact, but one that can be cited with certainty is in the area of communication. This challenge is mentioned in the New Testament.

In the third chapter of James's letter to the Jewish Christians who were scattered among the nations, he addresses the dangers of misusing the tongue. He identifies the tongue as a boaster, a fire starter, a source of iniquity, and a defiler. After going through his righteous rant about the potential harm that our tongues can do, James then offers what appears to be little hope: "No one can tame the tongue" (James 3:8).

When I first read James's blanket statement, I instantly felt depressed. I pushed my chair back, raised my hands in surrender, and said out loud, "Why tell me all this bad news about the tongue and then tell me that no one, not a single human, is able to tame it? Where's the hope in that?"

> The human tongue is like a tube of
> toothpaste—when squeezed by anger
> whatever's in it will come out.
>
> **Annie Chapman**

Thankfully, my despair turned to gladness when I thought of Ken's sage advice in light of what I'd just read. I realized that instead of being a verse with no hope, verse eight contained all the hope I needed. Again, I spoke aloud. "James is right. No one can control his tongue...without God's help. And Ken is right. God's got life rigged so I can't do it right without Him."

Since that wedding a few years ago, I've repeated Ken's words many times, and not just when I'm facing the challenge of taming my tongue. It's also helpful when I'm trying to deal effectively with fear, greed, selfishness, jealousy, anger, and a host of other areas of life that require the help of God to manage. For me—and for you too, I imagine—admitting often that God's got life rigged so we can't do it "right" without Him is a great step toward true and lasting joy.

Jesus said to them, "With people this is impossible, but with God all things are possible" (Matthew 19:26).

32

"Sometimes You Have to Let Your Feet Do the Talkin'"

This bit of timeless advice comes from the song entitled "Run!" The lyric states what I imagined one of my favorite Bible characters would say to all of us who find ourselves in situations where we are sexually tempted.

Run!

There was a man in the Bible named Joseph
If he were here, he would tell you it's true
It's not if, but it's when
Temptation's gonna come to me and you
He ought to know 'cause his boss's wife
Tried to get him into bed
He knew it wasn't right, and what he did instead
Tells us all
What we ought to do

"Run! Don't hesitate
Run! Don't negotiate
Hurry to the Father in the name of the Son
It's where you'll find the victory 'cause it's already won
When temptation comes

Go like a bullet from a gun
And run"

Oh brothers, when we're tempted just remember
The devil hates us when we tell him "No!"
He'll hold on as long as he can
Like the woman who had Joseph by his coat
But he did what he had to do
Let her have the coat he wore
Left her standin' in the room
He shot out the door, and he was gone
That's how he told her "No!"

Now can't you hear ol' Joseph sayin', "You gotta be smart
Sometimes you have to let your feet do the talkin' for your
heart!"

"You gotta run! Don't hesitate
Run! Don't negotiate
Hurry to the Father in the name of the Son
It's where you'll find the victory 'cause it's already won
When temptation comes
Go like a bullet from a gun
And run!"[8]

She caught him by his garment saying, "Lie with me!" And
he left his garment in her hand and fled, and went outside
(Genesis 39:12).

Run from anything that stimulates youthful lust (2 Timothy 2:22 NLT).

33

"The Masters Tournament Isn't the Place to Learn to Play Golf"

few summers ago I invested a hard-earned hundred bucks to
participate in a fund-raising golf "scramble" in support of a local
charity. For those who don't know what a scramble is, let me enlighten
you. It's played by teams of two, three, or four players. The team members advance the ball down the fairways using the best of the team's
shots. There were an unusual number of teams signed up for the charity tournament, which made it extra critical that the tee times were on
schedule and that each group played without unnecessary delay. All
was flowing well until the group in front of our foursome teed off.

One of the players on the team was everywhere on the course but
the fairway. His first shot ended up in the weeds on the right side. He
bee-lined it from the tee box to the rough. As he hacked around the
high grass using his iron like a sickle, it was obvious he wasn't familiar
with the courtesy of leaving the ball behind and dropping another for
the sake of time.

The second hole wasn't much different for the novice player, except
he went to the left rough for more weed-whacking. The comments
among our team, and I'm sure on the teams behind us, were turning
from mumbling to grumbling. I tried to be "sanctified" about the situation and keep my thoughts to myself, but finally I had to say what
was on my mind.

I stood with my group on the fourth tee waiting once again for the snail-paced group ahead of us to advance down the course, and it was clear by then that their meandering teammate was a first-timer. As I watched the wandering and wayward golfer go from rough to rough, I said, "The Masters Tournament isn't the place to learn how to play the game of golf!"

I didn't mean to imply that I, or anyone else on my team for that matter, was skilled enough to play the course in Augusta, Georgia, in April of each year with the pro golfers. What I meant was that in order for a golfer to contribute to the steady flow of play on any course, he or she should first take some lessons. The goal should be to at least get good enough at the game to be able to play it in a timely manner instead of being the wreck on the golf highway that blocks the traffic.

This bit of fairway wisdom applies to golf, but it can apply to other fields as well. One of them is music. I'm embarrassed to say that I've had the sad experience of being the hacker who held up a song. I'd written a radio jingle for a broadcast music company and was in the studio when they recorded the track for the 58-second commercial. The acoustic guitar player called in sick, so the session was short a player.

The owner of the company was also the producer of the recording, and he said to me, "Grab a guitar and get out there, Steve. We need you to play on this session." I gasped. I'd never played a Nashville "session" before in my life. The men in the room were highly skilled players, and I was just a songwriter who knew enough chords to play around my melodies.

I regret to say that the number of stops and start-overs that I caused were far more than what the pros in the room were used to. I have a mental list of some moments in my day I'd like to forget, and without exception my fumbling and stumbling guitar playing at the session is near the top. I can't blame the producer for throwing me under the musical bus because I should have been better prepared for the surprise call on my skills. As I look back, it makes me regret being so upset with that weed-whacker at the golf scramble.

34

"Confession Is Good for the Soul— Even If It Sends the Body to Jail"

The story was told about the owner of a small-town department store who closed and locked the doors behind him and then headed home for the evening. He didn't notice the two teenagers watching him as he got into his vehicle and drove away.

That night around midnight, the boys returned to the store. After breaking a window in the back door, they were able to get inside. The aisles were barely lit by the glow of the exit signs that were left on overnight, but they could see well enough to get what they wanted. After each of them helped themselves to some new tennis shoes, a nice jacket, a shiny watch, and a few other items that filled the bags they'd taken from the shelves, they hurried out and headed home.

When the owner returned the next morning and found that his store had been broken into, he was so upset and angry that he suffered a fatal heart attack. An employee, who arrived just after the owner, called the police. When the police arrived, the employee reported that she was convinced her boss's death was directly related to the trauma that was triggered by his discovery of the robbery.

It didn't take long for the news about the cause of the storeowner's demise to reach the ears of the boys who had broken into the store. The older boy immediately decided he would keep his mouth shut about being involved in order to avoid punishment. The younger one, however, was ridden with guilt. He personally knew the owner and his family, and his gut churned with regret. He was especially disgusted with himself because he'd allowed his partner in crime to talk him into participating.

For a couple of days, the younger boy wrestled with whether or not to turn himself in. Finally, he couldn't take the feelings of guilt any longer and walked to the police station. After confessing his involvement in the robbery he was escorted to a jail cell, where he would await the arrival of his parents as well as the churnings of the judicial system.

Sitting alone on the hard bed in the cell located in the basement of the station, the young man felt relieved that he'd come forward with the truth. There was consolation in knowing there would be no more need to hide his thoughts, no more worry about being found out, and, best of all, no more nausea the nagging guilt was causing.

Though it wasn't easy, he'd encountered a life-changing fact: Confession is good for the soul and freeing for the mind—even if it lands the body in jail.

35

"'Win or Lose' People Will Never Be as Happy as 'Right or Wrong' People"

We live in a world filled with at least two types of people. There are those who look at life through a "win or lose" attitude and those who see life from a "right or wrong" viewpoint. These two types are found in families, businesses, schools, politics, sports, and countless other settings.

"Win or lose" people can be merciless to others as they attempt to make themselves the winners and everyone else losers. To be the victor, "win or lose" people will sometimes do everything from lying to cheating, from slandering to even murdering to ensure they come out on top. The problem for most who live this way is that when they get to the top, they find that they're alone.

On the other hand, those who are driven by a sense of right and wrong are not as impressed with winning as they are with what is morally correct. In most cases, they are aware of and care that others will be affected by the outcome of their conduct.

Perhaps the best examples of these two types of people is found in the biblical account of David and Uriah (2 Samuel 11). In this well-known story, David sees Bathsheba moon-bathing one evening from his rooftop vantage point. He used his position as king to demand that she be brought to him. The result of this tryst was an unplanned pregnancy and a baby born out of wedlock.

David, who was unwilling to lose his respectable reputation, displayed a "win or lose" attitude when he attempted a cover up of his responsibility for the unborn child. He called Uriah in from the battlefield and tried to get him to spend the night with his wife, Bathsheba. The plan was for them to reconnect so Uriah would be named as the daddy.

But David didn't count on Uriah being motivated by a keen sense of right or wrong. The conniving king was quite upset when Uriah refused to enjoy his wife's company out of respect for his soldiers who were still on the front lines. With anger and revenge in his heart for his plans going awry, David next arranged for Uriah to be killed on the battlefield.

Uriah's choice to be a "right or wrong" person got him killed. David's decision to yield to a "win or lose" attitude was rewarded with results that were momentarily satisfying but ended up being far worse than dying honorably in war. He suffered the death of the baby born to Bathsheba. David also had to deal with the gut-churning realization that he'd offended God by his misuse of power, by feeding his adulterous desire, and by his murderous treatment of his loyal subject and soldier Uriah. But the story doesn't end there.

The good news is that God sent his prophet Nathan to David to rebuke him. David recognized what he did was wrong and repented of his terrible sin—and God forgave him. His contrite prayer is recorded in Psalm 51. Anyone who acknowledges their guilt of hurting someone through a "win or lose" attitude can also pray and ask God for forgiveness and mercy. If that's you, and you desire to get back to being a "right or wrong" person, take a moment to pray like David did. Forgiveness and peace will be yours.

> Be gracious to me, O God, according to
>   Your lovingkindness;
> According to the greatness of Your compassion
>   blot out my transgressions.
> Wash me thoroughly from my iniquity
>   And cleanse me from my sin.

For I know my transgressions,
    And my sin is ever before me.
Against You, You only, I have sinned
    And done what is evil in Your sight,
So that You are justified when You speak
    And blameless when You judge.

Behold, I was brought forth in iniquity,
    And in sin my mother conceived me.
Behold, You desire truth in the innermost being,
    And in the hidden part You will make me know
        wisdom.
Purify me with hyssop, and I shall be clean;
    Wash me, and I shall be whiter than snow.
Make me to hear joy and gladness,
    Let the bones which You have broken rejoice.
Hide Your face from my sins
    And blot out all my iniquities.

Create in me a clean heart, O God,
    And renew a steadfast spirit within me.
Do not cast me away from Your presence
    And do not take Your Holy Spirit from me.
Restore to me the joy of Your salvation
    And sustain me with a willing spirit.
Then I will teach transgressors Your ways,
    And sinners will be converted to You.
Deliver me from bloodguiltiness, O God, the
    God of my salvation;
Then my tongue will joyfully sing of Your righteousness
    (Psalm 51:1-14).

36

"Friends Help Sow Bad Seeds, but You Reap Alone"

I didn't realize how the conversation with my new Navy friend was growing in volume with each drink we downed. We were in a pub on a side street in a town on the coast of Italy. Until I climbed onto the bar stool next to him that night, this preacher's kid had never tasted alcohol. But my friend's description of the feelings that came with the honey-colored firewater created a curiosity that got the best of me.

After putting away a few glasses of the sweet and innocent tasting mixture of rum and Coke, I noticed the world was spinning around me. And because my tongue seemed as thick as a Nerf football, I felt like I had to talk louder to make the words come out. Somewhere in my muddled brain I thought, *My friend's right. This is fun!*

Then slowly but surely things changed inside my body. I started feeling like my stomach was being squeezed in a vise. I'm not sure how I made it to the bathroom before the heaving began, but I did even though my legs seemed to go wherever *they* wanted. As I knelt alone in the bathroom stall and spent several minutes dealing with the very disgusting taste of drunkenness, I remember feeling angry with my friend for not being there to help me stagger through this part of the experience. He was at my side and smiling big when the rum was going down, but he'd abandoned me when it was coming up.

If you have plenty of horse sense you'll
never lose money betting on humans.

W.C. Fields
(paraphrased)

I didn't see him again until the next day when our ship hoisted anchor and set sail for another port. I found out that he'd left me on my own because he didn't want to spend the rest of his night of liberty helping me get back to my bunk.

Though I feel embarrassed recounting my one-and-only-bout with being inebriated, I can at least say I learned a huge lesson that night in that Mediterranean port bathroom stall. No matter how many friends are around when I plant the sickening seeds of mischief, when it comes time to gather the crop I'll be all by myself in the field.

> Each one of us will give an account of himself to God (Romans 14:12).

37

"If You Don't Want It Repeated, Make Sure Kids Aren't Listening"

A mom and dad left their seven-year-old daughter with her uncle and his wife, who hadn't been married very long and didn't have any children. The parents' plan was to be gone for just a few days on a short business trip. This would also let the newlyweds get a taste of parenthood.

On the final morning of the daughter's stay with her kinfolk, they took her to swim in a local lake. As the uncle drove, his niece sat quietly in the backseat of the car. Suddenly he hit the brakes and came to a screeching stop.

When the girl sat up straight and looked over the front seat, she could see that someone had unexpectedly pulled out from a side street into the path of her uncle's car. As the driver pulled away, he offered a humble, "sorry about that" wave. It was obviously not enough to appease her uncle. He mashed the gas pedal, and in the same moment let out seat-shaking expletives about the man behind the wheel of the other car. His short-but-bitter verbal tirade was followed by a nonapproving tone in his wife's question: "Did you forget who's in the backseat?"

The uncle quickly glanced at his brother's little girl in the rearview mirror and saw that she seemed unfazed by the incident or his language. From what he could tell, she had no clue what he'd said about the driver of the other car. He felt relieved and confident that he hadn't done any damage to his young niece.

He could not have been more wrong.

The girl's parents returned late-Saturday afternoon and picked up their daughter. They headed home. The next morning, they climbed into the family van and headed to church. As her dad drove down the street where the church was located, an oncoming pickup truck suddenly made a turn in front of him. He had to slam on his brakes and slow to a near stop. When he did, he heard some words come from the backseat of his car that stunned him. He quickly looked at his wife who had heard them too. Her jaw was in her lap.

The mother nearly broke her neck as she quickly turned around and angrily said, "What did you just say, young lady?"

Their daughter sensed that something wrong had just happened. She nervously said the words again.

Bewildered by her daughter's willingness to repeat such unacceptable language, the mom asked, "Where did you hear that?"

Their daughter answered, "Oh, it's what Uncle Joe said the other day when a car pulled out in front us."

With that report, her exasperated mom and dad rolled their eyes and shook their heads. They knew what they were going to do.

That afternoon the guilty uncle got a call from his brother. The uncle was mortified that his niece had picked up his words, and he promised to be more careful with his tongue, especially when his niece was within earshot.

Before he hung up, the little girl's dad offered his brother a bit of wisdom that he was sure would help in the future when his own kids were in the backseat of his car. "Brother, you gotta remember: Kids might have little ears, but they have big mouths. If you don't want it repeated, don't say it when a kid is around."

How true!

> Let no unwholesome word proceed from your mouth, but only such a word as is good for edification according to the need of the moment, so that it will give grace to those who hear (Ephesians 4:29).

38

"Sometimes You Have to Turn a Third Cheek"

A church in Texas invited Annie and me to sing in their Sunday-morning service. On Saturday night, we checked into the very nice room they'd reserved for us at a fancy high-rise hotel. We got up early the next morning, and the plan was for me to go to the church to get a sound check and then come back to get Annie.

I headed out to our motor home. When I was in eyesight of our gas-powered house on wheels, I noticed that something didn't look right. I was shocked when I realized that the metal light pole I'd parked under was lying across the roof of "Big Ben" (the name we'd given to the rig because it groaned like a bear when we pushed the brake pedal). When I got very close to the vehicle, I could see that the damage was more than I first thought.

I slowly opened the door to look inside our comfortable vehicle and saw that the cluster of lights at the top of the pole had fallen through the roof. I could see daylight through the ceiling! And as if that were not enough devastation, the rain that had come with the windy storm had soaked the carpet and couches. I couldn't believe what I was seeing.

I closed the motor-home door and headed to the front desk in the main lobby of the hotel. When I described what I'd found in the parking lot to the lady behind the counter, she seemed to go into a coma. The blank stare I got was chilling. After I finished my damage report, she disappeared for a minute or so and then came back with a man in a suit. He sounded nervous when he invited me into his office.

Up to that point I had been nice and calm. However, when "the suit" started writing down a couple of phone numbers for me to call to connect with their main office the next day, I felt like I'd just been slapped on the cheek. I began to feel a boiling sensation in my blood. I could tell I was being put off, and I didn't like it one little bit. Then, with some obviously defensive language, the suit implied that I was probably thinking *lawsuit* and was hearing the sound of a cash register cha-chinging in my head. I felt like I'd been judged wrongly. From all indications, I was sure that my *other cheek* had just been slapped too.

As I sat across from the man and listened to his cold and wordy attempt to pass me off to his peeps somewhere in a city far away, I started mentally rehearsing the tirade that I wanted him to hear. I must admit that I also imagined myself standing up, crawling across his desk, and serving him a knuckle sandwich for breakfast. But I didn't—and there was a good reason for exercising some restraint.

Never pass up a good chance to
keep your mouth shut.
Annie Chapman

I assumed he knew that the folks paying for our room was a church just down the road. He was probably aware that I was one-half of the guest duo who would be singing in the Sunday service. That's likely what he knew, but what *I* knew was equally important.

In the unfortunate situation that had arisen, I was the face of the congregation that was hosting us. Whatever I did in that moment would reflect on the church organization, its people, and its leadership. Ultimately, I knew I was an ambassador of Christ, and my response to the disappointing and rude way I was being treated could have a lot to do with what the man might think of God and His followers.

So for those reasons I respectfully informed him that I felt the matter was a long way from being resolved. As politely as I could, I stood up, excused myself, and walked out.

I left the suit's office with the phone numbers he gave me to call the next morning, but that wasn't all I took with me. I left with firsthand knowledge of what to do when someone slaps me on one cheek, and then slaps the other cheek that I turn toward them. In that instance I had to use yet another cheek God gave me by turning and walking away. By doing so, I managed to not only stay out of jail as a result of being arrested for mashing the man's nose, but I didn't stain the reputation of the local church or the name of Christ.

In case you're wondering what happened with our rolling home, it took a full three months of wrangling with the hotel's insurance company adjuster to process the repair of our critically injured motor home. In the meantime, they agreed to rent replacement units for us whenever we were scheduled to travel until the restoration was complete. What they didn't realize was how busy we were at the time. Nearly every weekend for the next three months we took trips in some really nice motor homes and a few plush conversion vans. I felt that my decision to turn a third cheek to the suit had been rewarded.

> Turn from evil and do good; seek peace and pursue it (Psalm 34:14 NIV).

"What Others Think About You Is None of Your Business"

O n one of our concert trips quite a while ago, the auditorium where the event was held was a beautiful, well-equipped room. An audio technician and a pair of young stagehands were assigned to help us. Their presence was a very welcome luxury because we didn't often get to enjoy the assistance of an on-site crew.

The doors opened and the seats filled with people from the area. We were pleasantly surprised by the turnout. The response from the audience was most encouraging too.

Our kids were teenagers at the time, and Nathan usually ran the sound for us. Because we were using the concert venue's personnel for audio mixing, he had the night off. His only responsibility was to join us on stage for a couple of songs in the second half, along with his sister, Heidi. Other than that, he was free to hang out in the green room during the concert.

One of the crewmembers sat stage-left behind the curtain and communicated with the sound man in the balcony control booth via their headsets as we performed. Our son happened to walk by him and heard one side of the conversation and noted some muffled laughter. When he wandered over to the other side of the stage and saw another headset that wasn't being used, curiosity got the best of him. He decided to see if he could hear the exchanges between the stagehand and the sound booth tech.

He placed the headset on and quietly eavesdropped. He listened for a few minutes then angrily ripped the headset off and headed to the green room. During the break, Annie and I went there and found him pacing the floor with his hands in his pockets. We had seen that behavior before and knew something major was on his mind.

"What's up, son?" I asked.

"You won't believe what I heard the stagehand say to the sound man!"

I pulled up a folding chair and sat down to listen.

"I heard the stagehand say to his buddy upstairs, 'Can you believe anyone came to hear these people? I don't get it. Totally boring.'"

Of course, I had to ask. "How did you hear what was said?"

"I heard it over the headphone system they use. I listened in."

My astute wife, who is also a very wise mother, offered her input. "Son, first of all, now you know why eavesdropping isn't a really good idea. Sometimes you hear things you don't want to hear. Second, what someone thinks of us is actually none of our business. They're entitled to whatever they want to think. It doesn't do you any good to know what they said, and it doesn't do us any good either."

The best way to curse the darkness
is to light a candle.

Jim Bakker

Annie's words didn't immediately squelch the ire our son was fighting, and quite honestly, I was feeling it with him. However, I wanted us both to get over hearing such a slam on us, so I got an idea. I'd learned a long time ago that a good way to win these kinds of battles is to, as the Bible says, "heap burning coals" on their heads by covering the offenders with kindness (Romans 12:20 NIV).

When the break was over, I stepped up to the mic and said, "By the way, before we go any further tonight, let me thank the sound man upstairs and the stage crew backstage for all their great help. This evening would not be a success without them."

Nathan stood backstage as he heard me speak. He could see the face of the stagehand who had spoken disparaging words about us. My son told me later that the guy's expression was one of shock. Nathan guessed that he knew that somehow he'd been busted. Whether or not he knew that his unkind remarks were overheard, we'll never know. But I do know for sure that our son learned a valuable lesson that evening that has served him well.

> Don't eavesdrop on the conversation of others. What if the gossip's about you and you'd rather not hear it? (Ecclesiastes 7:21 MSG).

40

"Renaming Sin to Avoid Spiritual Stink Is like Painting an Outhouse"

The list of sinful behaviors that have been renamed in attempts to soften or remove the reality of their ugly effects on our culture is disturbingly long. Here are some examples of how redefining sin is done on an everyday basis, along with the truth behind the camouflage.

- "Our state congressman was picked up for a DUI after leaving a *highly respected gentleman's club*." [He got pulled over for driving while dangerously drunk after leaving a strip club.]

- "There were 200 people at the *pro-choice rally* yesterday." [200 people want the public to know they support the slaughter of innocent unborn babies.]

- "The school principal lost his job when he was caught with *child pornography*." [The principal used pictures of children being sexually abused and exploited as a source of entertainment and gratification.]

- "My son just *moved in* with his girlfriend." [He and his girlfriend are living as a married couple without God's blessing.]

- "She dropped out of college to become an *exotic dancer*." [She became a stripper.]

- "The politician *misspoke* when he said he had no part in the illegal land deal." [He lied.]

- "She announced on the news that she embraces an *alternate lifestyle*." [She announced she's homosexual.]

- "The pastor was caught in an *extra-marital affair*." [He committed adultery.]

- "It was a great movie—except for the language." [If you go see it, you've been warned that you'll likely hear God's name abused and demeaned.]

Here are a few more recognizable attempts to verbally sugarcoat sin.

- "He was guilty of *domestic violence*." [He beat and abused his wife.]

- "He used an *escort service*." [He hired a prostitute.]

- "She eats *compulsively*." [She's a glutton.]

- "She's *ambitiously challenged*." [She's lazy.]

- "He was convicted of *distributing an illegal substance*." [He's a drug dealer.]

- "The boy found his dad's *adult material*." [The boy found his dad's stash of pornography.]

- "Be careful what you tell her because she *can't keep a secret*." [She's a gossip.]

- "He's got a *short fuse*." [He doesn't control his anger.]

Like a friend says about renaming sin, "You can call poop puddin' if you want to, but it's still gonna stink."

> Woe to those who call evil good, and good evil; who substitute darkness for light and light for darkness; who substitute bitter for sweet and sweet for bitter! Woe to those who are wise in their own eyes and clever in their own sight! (Isaiah 5:20-21).

41

"Percentages Don't Have to Add Up to Reveal Important Truths"

Percentages can be mathematically warped, but there can still be hints of good advice. You'll also find a smidgen of wisdom in the following statements that are also a little skewed.

- 98 percent of becoming a CPA is wanting to; the other 10 percent is having good math skills.

- 10 percent of becoming a youth pastor is wanting to; the other 110 percent is liking young people.

- 99 percent of becoming a professional rock climber is developing muscle strength; the other 200 percent is honestly answering the question, "Why?"

- Only 7 percent of communication is words; the other 98 percent is saying them again.

- 50 percent of safely flying an airplane is training; the other 500 percent is knowing what to do when the houses are quickly getting bigger.

- 3 percent of learning to ride a unicycle is practicing; the other 100 percent is whether or not you can afford health insurance.

- 85 percent of riding a vicious rodeo bull for more than 8 seconds is hanging on; the other 99 percent rarely do.

- 99.9 percent of having a new car is wishing and shopping for it; the other 21.5 percent is applied in interest on a monthly basis.

42

"If You Keep Giving, Don't Be Surprised When They Want More"

My friend Sam was part of a hard-working music group that started gaining a lot of media attention. The radio airplay given to their songs, their packed concert schedule, and the growing number of TV appearances caused their business to expand so much that it was necessary to hire some help to manage the success.

As the leader of the group, Sam had the time-consuming task of searching for their needed assistants. Within a couple of weeks, he'd recruited a pair of employees. After about three months, the additional team had grown to four employees working in rented office space.

Sam was an unusually generous soul, but his big-heartedness didn't serve him well as an employer. Instead of paying a wage that was appropriate for the positions, he chose a pay scale that was very liberal. The way he figured it, if they were really happy about the amount of their checks, they'd be happier to come in every day and do the work.

> If you loan money to a friend,
> you risk losing both.
>
> **Annie Chapman**

A few months went by before Sam discovered that his "if you give 'em more, you'll get more" approach wasn't working well. Unfortunately, he learned this hard lesson when he overheard one of his helpers make a statement not meant for the boss's ears. Sam was standing just out of eyesight when one employee said to another, "These guys are making a lot more money than their help is. They ought to share it with us!"

In that moment, Sam realized he had a problem on his hands. For the first time, he encountered a trait in human nature that can often surface when a person is consistently given more for work than they've actually earned. While overpaying a person might initially result in their thankfulness and contribute to a stronger work ethic, in far too many cases the benefit is temporary…at best. Whether it was caused by greed or jealousy (or likely both), there came a time when the gratitude that Sam's employee felt turned to resentment because he didn't see his boss's generosity increase with the band's growing success.

Sadly, the unhappy employee didn't keep his resentment to himself. Sam found out that his poisonous attitude was being passed on to others in the office. To keep a team that was strong, the disgruntled employee was dismissed and replaced, with the replacement being paid a salary that matched the position. Live and learn.

43

"Let 'Em Be Boys"

At the time of this writing there are four does and one buck in our "GrandChap herd." The boy is fifth in the line of grand blessings, and it's quite amazing how different he is from our granddaughters. While it can sometimes be exhausting at our age to chase him through our house and around our yard for the sake of keeping him safe, it is an absolute delight to see how rambunctious he is.

My hope is to always be able to do what I can to cultivate his very active nature, and there's a good reason for it as explained in this lyric written with my friend Dana Bacon, who is also granddad to some very energetic grandsons.

Let 'Em Be Boys

She held her breath and watched her son
She didn't get it. "Where is the fun
In climbin' so high up in that tree?"
And his daddy just stood there
She said, "That oak looks a hundred feet tall,
I'm so afraid that he's gonna fall"
His daddy said, "Don't worry; he'll be OK
He's gotta do it; God made him that way!"

Let 'em be boys
Let 'em be boys

They need to get a little dirt on
They need to make some noise
Turn 'em loose…and let 'em run
Don't you know—boys is where men come from?
Oh, let 'em be boys

His daddy said, "I think it's time
We let him pick a Daisy—the shootin' kind
A Red Ryder, that's what he needs!"
And his mama just stood there
She gave that look; didn't have to say a word
"He'll shoot his eye out," that's what he heard
He said, "Oh, baby, it's easy to explain
Our kid was born with BBs in his veins"

Let 'em be boys
Let 'em be boys
They need to get a little dirt on
They need to make some noise
Turn 'em loose…and let 'em run
Don't you know boys is where men come from?
Oh, let 'em be boys

Let 'em play
'Cause that's the way they'll get stronger
They gotta be tough
When they grow up and the world is sittin' on their
    shoulders[9]

44

"God's Gifts Are Meant to Be Given Away"

One of the greatest guitar players of our time, and arguably of all time, is Phil Keaggy. His ability is celebrated by anyone who has ever heard him. (Amazingly, he plays with just nine fingers due to an accident when he was very young.) It's been said about his guitar playing, "If you don't know how to play and you hear Phil, it'll make you want to learn. But if you do play, it'll make you want to quit." That pretty much explains how incredibly talented he is. But as awesome as Phil is on guitar, I can personally report that he is very generous with his God-given talent.

Previously I shared about our son, Nathan, and his high school project to plan, perform, and carry out the filming of a music video. I helped by funding the event and taking care of a few other details. What Nathan didn't know was that I also called Phil. Because Nathan was such a huge fan of his style, I asked Phil if he could join Nathan on stage for one song.

Phil's schedule was wall-to-wall, but he saw an opportunity to encourage a budding guitarist. For that reason, he graciously agreed to participate. When he walked into the studio carrying his electric guitar case, everyone was shocked—especially Nathan. The song the two of them played together turned out to be a highlight of the evening and a priceless musical memory, to say the least.

When Phil left the event, he had no way of knowing that he'd just shared the stage with a young man who would put the encouragement he'd received to good use. Nathan went on to use his music gift professionally, and I can add that he's impacted an entire genre of music through his skills.

For Phil, someone of such renown in the world of music, to have chosen to invest in our son told me a lot about the man. It's obvious that Phil embraces the fact that the gift God gave him to play music will always be just that—a gift he can share with others.

In addition to musical talent, there are other gifts that God gives all of us…with the intention that they be shared. Love, hope, encouragement, strength, patience, along with mechanical and mathematical expertise, the ability to teach, and other occupational skills are just to name a few. There is one gift that is most important of all. When God "gave His only begotten Son" to mankind, we were given the gift that is above all gifts (John 3:16). Those who accept Jesus and believe in Him are promised eternal life with Him. Oh, what a marvelous gift to have to share with others.

> As each one has received a special gift, employ it in serving one another as good stewards of the manifold grace of God. Whoever speaks, is to do so as one who is speaking the utterances of God; whoever serves is to do so as one who is serving by the strength which God supplies; so that in all things God may be glorified through Jesus Christ, to whom belongs the glory and dominion forever and ever. Amen (1 Peter 4:10-11).

45

"Just Between You and Me and the Fence Post"

If you would have told me back when I was a 15-year-old that time would come when, with the touch of a pad, I could send my thoughts, a still picture, or a video of me to the entire world, I would have said, "You're nuts." Obviously, I would have been as wrong as $2 + 2 = 5$. I often hear the statement, "It's nothing short of amazing that technology has advanced to the point that we now have the ability to communicate on such a vast, global scale and with speed that boggles the brain." I agree, but not totally. Saying that something has advanced is to imply that it has improved. In the case of technology, I'm not so sure that saying it has "advanced" is a worthy assessment. In my estimation, communication technology would be considered improved only if the privacy level had stayed the same as it was prior to the immense technology expansion.

I'm amazed and grateful that I can tell a college student on the other side of the world via email that I'm sending him a care package filled with homemade goodies, books, and music. Though the items might not be all that valuable to anyone but the student, I'm not fond of the idea that potentially anyone on the planet can hack into that message and know what's in the box.

> When you throw a rock into a crowd of
> dogs, the one that gets hit will bark.
>
> **Author unknown**

What makes the so-called advancement of communication technology a concern is the risk I take if I included in my email that something of greater value was in the box, such as cash, a credit card, or even some confidential documents. To think that that information is potentially visible to anyone in the world is cause to worry. What's worse is that I'm not convinced it would be safer these days to alert the student by phone that the package and its important contents was on the way.

The bottom line is that the old saying "just between you and me and a fence post" no longer applies because that fence post may be a cell tower posing as a piece of rough-cut pine. I don't want to sound overly paranoid, but I'm wondering if anything that needs to be said in private to someone these days is best said with a cupped hand between my lips and that person's ear—and without my microphone-equipped cell phone in my shirt pocket.

> Set a guard, O LORD, over my mouth; keep watch over the
> door of my lips (Psalm 141:3).

"'Goodbye' or 'I'll See You Again'?"

While attending a birthday celebration for my dad, I was privileged to meet the pastor of the congregation my folks had started attending a few months earlier. I learned that the full-time vocation for the preacher was not the pulpit. Instead, he was a mortician by trade. During our conversation, I discovered that he views his dual role as pastor and funeral director as a "double opportunity" to share the good news of salvation through Jesus Christ. He was quick to say, though, that he does share with necessary differences in his approach.

"If I'm in the pulpit at a regularly scheduled church service," he said, "I'm very straightforward with the message of the gospel. When I'm asked, however, to stand in as the clergy at a wake or a funeral, I have to be careful to not take advantage of the vulnerable state the family members and friends of the deceased are in." He went on to say, "While I don't believe it's appropriate at all to go 'hellfire and brimstone' on folks at a funeral, I do think it's important to remind them that there is something to consider that has eternal significance. My goal is simply to get folks to think about their spiritual condition."

When he told me how he managed to discreetly sow the seeds of the gospel into the hearts of those he served as a preacher/mortician, I heard a song idea. In the refrain of the following lyric you'll read what this gentle and caring man says to all those present when he's filling the role of preacher at a funeral. When he's simply standing by as the funeral director near the casket as individuals move through the viewing line, he prayerfully considers who might need to hear his words and offers them quietly. His message is definitely wisdom worth passing on—and not just to those who are grieving. We can all use this reminder.

You Can Choose

They gathered in the service
For a dad who passed away
The preacher spoke about the hope—
A reunion some sweet day

Then with love so kind and tender
In a voice broken by tears
He said these words meant to be heard
By the wayward ones who were there

"You can choose to tell your loved one 'goodbye'
Or you can tell them 'I'll see you again'
It's up to you
What will you choose?
Will it be 'goodbye' or
'Someday I will see you again'?"

There was silence for a moment
Then everyone heard the sound
The cries of a son—the dad's only one
Who was lost and yet to be found

He stood up; went down to the altar
Fell to his knees and prayed
Then he said, "God, tell my dad, I know he'll be glad,
That I heard that preacher say…

"'You can choose to tell your loved one "goodbye"
Or you can tell them "I'll see you again"

It's up to you
What will you choose?
Will it be "goodbye" or
"someday I will see you again" '?"[10]

The Lord Himself will descend from heaven with a shout, with the voice of the archangel and with the trumpet of God, and the dead in Christ will rise first. Then we who are alive and remain will be caught up together with them in the clouds to meet the Lord in the air, and so we shall always be with the Lord (1 Thessalonians 4:16-17).

47

"God Made Babies Cute for a Reason"

As the due date for our firstborn approached, I suppose it was the excitement and anticipation I felt that hid the reality of what was about to happen. When our son was born, our tidy little duplex went from spotless to spit up, from the aroma of strawberry incense to the smell of you know what. Our world had been invaded, and we were in the midst of "Poopageddon." I had no idea that a human so tiny could create such disorder. But the truth be told, I didn't mind the mess at all.

When I looked at our new little buck and held him in my arms, nothing else in the world mattered, including the clutter and chaos that came with him. I was all smiles as I happily removed the heavily soiled cotton diapers off his little body and stuffed them barehanded in the bag for the "Dyddie Service" truck to pick up. The aura on our infant's angelic face somehow made my olfactory system accept only the sweet aroma of baby powder.

Having experienced such an incredible altered state known as "first-time fatherhood," I eventually came to the conclusion that God knew He had to make babies cute and adorable; otherwise, who in their right mind would put up with their messes?

48

"It Takes a Penny to Make a Dollar"

I was standing in line at a fast-food joint waiting to order a cup of "old people" coffee, when I saw a teenager in front of me drop a penny. Though he watched it fall to the floor and land near his feet, he made no effort to bend over and pick it up. I waited to see if the teen would retrieve the single coin. After a half-minute or so passed without him doing so, I made the assumption that he had no plans to reclaim it. As he was served the burger and fries he'd ordered, I stooped down and picked up the coin.

Before the teenager left the counter, I tapped him on the shoulder to get his attention. When he turned around, I held the coin up and offered him a little bit of fatherly advice. "Young man, I think you're aware that you dropped this penny. Did you know that it takes a penny to make a dollar? Without it, all you have is 99 cents."

As he took the coin and slid it into his pocket, he said, "I guess I never thought of a penny being worth all that much. I reckon you're right, and I'll keep it in mind."

I hoped I helped the youngster gain an appreciation for the significance of a single cent. Even more importantly, I hoped my penny's worth of wisdom will someday help him see that while some things might seem to have little value on their own, their contribution to the whole is vital.

For example, when he gets old enough to go to the polls during an election, perhaps his hearing of "it takes a penny to make a dollar" will help him understand how vital every vote is that's cast. Or if the chance comes for him to give a few dollars to a charity, maybe he'll realize that his small gift, when added to other donations, can make a huge difference to the cause.

The best way to lower the national income tax rate is for every employee to be paid in cash. But before receiving it, they have to stand and watch their employer count out the taxes to be withheld.

Rush Limbaugh
(paraphrased)

To this day, if I see a penny on the ground, on a street, on the pavement in a parking lot, or on the floor of a restaurant, I'm not going to let it lie there. I'll pick it up and smile knowing that I'm on my way to having another dollar.

49

"Good Tired vs. Bad Tired"

During an interview in the later part of the 1970s, singer/song-writer Harry Chapin quoted something his paternal grandfather, James Chapin, said. The following is a very trimmed paraphrase of his words: "Harry, when you work on your dreams all day, you might go home really tired—but it's a good tired. If you work on someone else's dreams all day—now, that's a bad tired."

Since the first time I heard the elder Mr. Chapin's insight offered to his grandson, I've not forgotten the impact of it. I can say that I have lived both sides of the statement. When I was 16, I swept the aisles of a dime store owned by a friend's dad. When I was 19, I was a yeoman in the Navy who helped a hard-nosed chief climb the promotion ladder. In my early twenties, I worked on the cleanup crew of a construction company that wasn't mine and stocked shoes in a giant footwear distribution center owned by a Nashville corporation. I've known how it feels to go to bed at night feeling the "bad tired."

I don't say the tiredness I felt was bad because my efforts were worthless. Of course, the income was important since it helped provide food, clothes, shelter, and transportation. It was a bad tired because at the end of the day the only thing I had to show for my work was having helped someone else feel "the good tired." When it came to reaching the end of my days and enjoying a sense of fulfillment in the way that Mr. Chapin implied, I didn't feel it. At least not until I did something similar to what he did.

James Chapin was a painter with a moderate amount of commercial success. Though he wished he would have achieved more, he said he felt completely satisfied by being able to do nothing else but paint every day. His report about how right it felt for him to do what he had to do to spend his time doing only what he loved to do, was the kind of testimony that tempted me to leave my paying job and risk starvation for the sake of music.

Thankfully, however, I had folks around me who advised me to not go full-time as a singer/songwriter until the invitations to perform grew in number to the point that I was "forced to retire," so to speak, from a nine-to-five job. Being a young husband and a soon-to-be dad, I knew they were right. I'm glad to say that the time eventually came in the latter part of the 1970s when I was able to write and perform for a living. And I'm grateful to say that since then I have not gone to bed a single night feeling the bad tired.

The work of their hands brings them reward (Proverbs 12:14 NIV).

50

"Little Boys and Big Hammers Are a Dangerous Combination"

I can think of at least two examples why it's not a good idea to let a little boy have a big hammer. The first one is named Billy. While he and his family were visiting his grandparents at their farm, his mother let him go outside and explore the premises. The shed next to the barn looked inviting, so the boy checked it out.

Inside the building was an array of tools. Included in the collection was a wooden-handled hammer. Billy grabbed it, stepped outside, and saw a tractor sitting nearby. Though it was one of his granddad's most dependable machines, as with most tractors on an active farm, the caked dirt on the wheels, the dents and scratches, and the greasy engine made it look broken down and abandoned to the young fellow from the city.

With hammer in hand, Billy climbed up on the massive red machine and sat down on the tattered seat covering. He looked over the half-dozen gauges on the open-air dash and saw that one of the glass coverings was cracked. Assuming it would be okay to make the others look the same on what he thought was a dilapidated old tractor, Billy took the hammer and began smashing the glass in each gauge. It was about that time that his grandfather came driving up in his truck.

His grandpa saw what his grandson was doing and quickly jumped out of his pickup, but it was too late. Billy had already broken every piece of round glass he could find on the tractor dash. He'd proven that a little boy with a hammer can be trouble looking for a place to happen.

The second example is our son, Nathan. When he was four years old, he found one of my hammers and wandered outside with it. I went out to find him and discovered he'd broken all of the basement windows he could reach with his newfound toy. I asked him why he'd done such a destructive thing, and his answer still haunts his mother and me to this day: "You never told me not to!"

We now have a grandson, and because I have a tractor and our house has windows, you can be sure that my hammer is hanging on a nail high up on the wall behind a locked shop door.

51

"If They Believe in You, They'll Invest in You"

An aspiring writer called me one day to get some advice about a decision he was making. After nearly three years, he'd finished the text for his first book. He'd sent it to a couple of publishers for their consideration. One of them called and went on and on about how good he thought the manuscript was. Then he popped the proposal.

"For only $4000," the publisher's agent promised, "I'll print a thousand copies and send 100 of them to various reviewers, radio and TV program directors, and other venues for the purpose of promotion. As the author, you will retain 50 percent of the rights to your book. The other half will be held by me in perpetuity."

My response? "My friend, the key word in all that you were told is '*perp*.' In my opinion, you got a call from a crook. If he was serious about how great he thinks your book is, he would offer *you* cash for the privilege of representing it." I heard only silence for a few seconds from the other end of the line. I knew I had sucked the wind out of my friend's sails, but I also knew I was offering him the best advice I could give. To cushion the blow of my response, I added, "My warning has nothing to do with whether or not your book is good. Instead, it's a matter of being smart and not letting your longing to be published make you blind to those who prey on people with dreams. Keep sending your book to publishers, and wait for the one who calls with both compliments and cash to back up what they tell you."

You can't make an old friend—
you can only grow one.

Author unknown

As it turned out, that's exactly what he did. And when he got the call I'd suggested he wait for, he was ecstatic. Needless to say I was thrilled as well when I got word that his yet-to-be-published book had found a home.

52

"It's Hard to Like Someone You Need When You Don't Like Why You Need Them"

A husband began losing the use of his muscles at age 42. The debilitating disease that stole his good health came at a time when he was being most productive with his skills as a carpenter. Within a few months he went from being totally independent and able to be the breadwinner to being completely dependent on others to help him through the day.

Because of his inability to perform the skills he'd possessed, his wife had to step in and find a job to support the two of them. Consequently, her absence from early in the morning to late in the day required her to enlist the services of someone to care for her disabled husband.

She chose a young man to come to their home from a local residential care business. He was her choice because he was strong and able to maneuver the wheelchair that her husband occupied most of the time, and he also had a pleasant demeanor to go along with his strength.

Though the young assistant's good attitude and abilities were the very things that were needed, there was trouble on the home front. At the end of each day, the young man would report to the wife that he'd endured lots of scolding from her husband. In addition, he said that when it came to bathing and feeding, all he heard was constant complaining. He alerted her that he wasn't sure if he could take much more of the confrontations.

The wife struggled to understand why the young hired help got so much mean-spirited resistance from her husband, who had been so good-natured before the disease attacked him. She prayed for wisdom about the situation. One day it dawned on her why he was acting the way he was. It wasn't because he didn't like the nice young man who was with him through the day; it was because he hated the reason the young man was there.

When she explained to the hired assistant that it wasn't him personally that her husband didn't like, everything changed. The young man revised his approach to helping by showing an extra measure of patience when her husband resisted him at mealtimes and during other tasks, such as changing his clothes and changing channels on the TV. He also learned that asking for advice on how to fix things around the house opened up some conversations that seemed to distract the once-active carpenter from his disability.

Eventually the two men became good friends. This wouldn't have happened if his loving wife hadn't cared enough to prayerfully think the matter through.

> Two are better than one because they have a good return for their labor. For if either of them falls, the one will lift up his companion. But woe to the one who falls when there is not another to lift him up (Ecclesiastes 4:9-10).

53

"You Can't Be Pitiful and Powerful at the Same Time"

I answered the phone one morning, and the voice of the person who responded to my hello sounded weak and tearful. The caller was a female friend of ours, and I had an immediate feeling that I wasn't the one she wanted or needed to talk to. I pressed the speaker to my chest and whispered the caller's name to Annie. I also made a sad face as I handed the phone to her so she could quickly prepare for the gloomy news I assumed she was about to hear.

As I listened to Annie's side of the conversation, I could easily tell our friend was nursing some emotional wounds. She'd just discovered that her husband had been seeing another woman for the past few months. I felt sorrow for our friend and was instantly upset with her husband. Not only was a marriage in jeopardy as a result of his unfaithfulness, but there were four young children who would have to deal with the fear of their family disintegrating and the gnawing disappointment they would feel toward their dad.

For the next 30 minutes Annie consoled our friend. I was quietly prayerful as my wife talked the hurting wife off the ledge of despair. Near the end of their exchange, I heard Annie say something I'd never heard her say. "Betty, you need to take charge of this situation. You gotta let Bob see some strength in your character to let him know you're not gonna be begging him for his devotion. Wipe your tears, put on some makeup, raise your head, and fight the urge to blame yourself and go around weepy and pitiful. It's not attractive to your husband, and the woman he's seeing doesn't need to see you that way either. It simply won't help matters." Then Annie said the words that I logged away in my memory and determined to remember them if I'm ever in a situation that requires me to show some resolve. She said, "You can't be pitiful and powerful at the same time."

As she delivered that closing bit of advice I could almost see our friend's shoulders straightening and her chin rising with the hope that she could handle the rough road that was ahead. I was sure she was feeling some needed courage as she heard insights on how to face her husband who had damaged her trust in him.

While there's no guarantee that all situations will have a similar outcome, as it turned out, our friend's husband stopped seeing the other woman and with the help of some pastoral counseling, the couple began the long journey to the restoration of their relationship. I'm convinced that Annie's sage advice contributed to the result.

> Be strong and let your heart take courage, all you who hope
> in the LORD (Psalm 31:24).

54

"You Just Never Know What a Day Will Bring"

My friend Lindsey Williams and I enjoy the challenge of hunting, but game animals are not all we like to pursue. We also like to get in a room and chase song lyrics. For that reason, we scheduled a meeting at a central location on Music Row in Nashville.

The day before we were to get together for co-writing, I got word of the tragic death of the son of a friend due to a highway accident. The shocking news was heavy on my heart the next day as I drove to the writing session with Lindsey. I thought of how the dad woke up the day before and had no idea that he would get such a devastating phone call about his son. With that scene in mind, I scribbled some words onto a piece of paper that was in my pocket. I hoped the idea might be good for the subject of a song.

When Lindsey and I met in the room, the first thing he asked me was if I'd heard about the accident. He knew the dad as well. "I've been thinking this morning about what a total shock the news must have been to the family and how their day was so unexpectedly filled with such sadness. I'm thinking maybe we should write a song about how we never know what will happen in a day. The title could be "You Just Never Know."

Chill bumps rose on my arms when I heard the song subject and

title Lindsey suggested. I reached into my pocket and handed the little piece of paper to him. "Can you read what I scribbled as I drove in
this morning?"

He read it aloud: "You Just Never Know."

We looked at each other for a couple of seconds and then started
unpacking our guitars. By lunchtime, we'd penned the following lyric
that addresses the ancient-but-timeless truth presented in Proverbs 27,
verse 1: "Do not boast about tomorrow, for you do not know what a
day may bring forth."

You Just Never Know

His hands on the wheel, radio on
Drivin' to work at the break of dawn
All at once up ahead, a car overturns
He's first on the scene, as it starts to burn
No time for thinking…life on the line
Now that mom and her baby are gonna be fine

You just never know what a day will bring
No way to know till it's happening
You can plan everything; you can hope, you can dream
But till the day comes and goes
You just never know

She gets on the plane…takes her seat
She calls home before it's time to leave
Tells her husband I'll be landing at noon
Can't wait to hold you…I'll see you soon
Then she bows her head as the big engines start
Whispers a prayer, then she crosses her heart

'Cause you just never know what a day will bring
No way to know till it's happening
You can plan everything; you can hope, you can dream

But till the day comes and goes
You just never know

Sometimes life can lift up your soul
Sometimes life can lay you low
Not much is certain but one thing is clear
You can't live in the moment till it gets here[11]

"You Can't Eat Everything in Sight and Still Like the Sight in the Mirror"

In my early teens I battled the dreaded skin scourge of acne. I spent years and a lot of my folks' cash fighting the unwelcomed bumps on my face with medicated pads and pastes. I was so desperate for deliverance from pimples I even tried—brace yourself for this news—liquid Lysol. I can personally report that after applying a strong disinfectant to the face, the result will not be the disappearance of inflamed bumps. Instead, you'll get a full-faced, red mass of flaming third-degree embarrassment that will make family and friends look with horror and ask two deserved questions: "Does that hurt?" and "What were you thinking?"

Thankfully, I didn't do any permanent damage to my face with the Lysol, but I didn't see any relief from the acne battle until a couple of years after I joined the Navy. While stationed on an aircraft carrier, I noticed my face was clearing. It may have been a matter of timing, in that I got old enough to grow out of the bane of acne, or it might have been the healing effects of being around salty air and water that caused the difference. Whatever caused it, I was grateful that the healing came. But with the clearing skin came an unexpected struggle.

Through the years of battling the bumps, one thing I did with great diligence was not eat certain types of foods that seemed to contribute to the problem. I had sworn off anything with chocolate, white sugar, heavy starches, and grease. What I didn't realize was how much healthier my self-imposed dietary restrictions was for the rest of my body. I was as skinny as a drinking straw. I didn't have an ounce of unnecessary fat on me. The inadvertent slimness, however, started disappearing when I reintroduced all the goodies I'd been saying no to for so long.

To test my new, smooth face one day, I intentionally ate a single Hershey bar that was sold in the ship's canteen. My eyes rolled back in my head with pleasure when the chocolate hit my tongue. I carefully watched the mirror for the two days that followed. When no white-top eruptions appeared, I tested the tasty treat again.

When I was finally convinced that my face wouldn't react to the "bad" stuff, I started stuffing the bad stuff in. I spent a good hunk of my paycheck on all the brands of candy bars I hadn't enjoyed since my early teens. I went through the chow line and piled on the grease-drenched French fries and helped myself to whatever else on the menu was drowned in lard. Most gratifying of all, I started eating white bread by the loaf.

A prideful man and a beagle are similar—they
both start eating without giving thanks.

Author unknown

About six months went by, and one day I noticed that all my Navy blue-and-white uniforms had shrunk. I thought one of my sailor buddies had taken all my pants and moved the button at the waist two inches to the left as a prank. My jaws began to swell, and my thighs grew tighter in my britches.

About a year later something woke me up to the fact that I'd been eating with abandonment. It happened the day I looked into a mirror and saw a heavyset guy looking back at me. I went to the clinic that was on the ship and asked to use the scales. I was shocked to discover I had gone from a Barney Fife-sized 140 pounds to a 210-pound Barnacle Bill the Sailor size. But unlike the cartoon character whose muscles were tight and well defined, I'd become a flabby swabbie.

It took more time than I wanted, but eventually I managed to regain control over my food intake. After a couple of years of being calorically careful, I got back to a size and weight that was healthy for my six-foot frame. Ever since then, I try to stay mindful of the fact that I can't eat everything in sight and expect to like what I see when I look in a mirror.

> Have you found honey? Eat only what you need (Proverbs 25:16).

56

"Why Pay Retail When You Can Pay Yard Sale?"

Annie was talking with a young couple and discovered that she shared a mutual preference in regard to making purchases for children. In their case, they were buying for their one-year-old son and soon-to-be-born daughter while Annie shopped for our five grandchildren, all under ten years old. The common ground she stood on with the young parents was that both of them rarely went to retail stores for the good deals. Instead, they were huge fans of yard sales.

Annie especially enjoyed swapping shopping exploits with the young parents and sharing them with me. One mother, for example, was actually giddy as she told about finding a yard filled with beautiful dresses that her daughter could eventually use. For a mere $20 she took home two bags filled with enough frilly things for their little girl to wear for the next two years.

One dad told about finding his little boy some tough-built toys that would last a long time, and that he paid with quarters instead of his credit card. He was especially proud of finding a brand-new pair of patent leather shoes for his daughter for a mere two dollars. He said they weren't only an expensive brand, but they were obviously unused. He smiled mischievously. "They looked like church shoes for an atheist."

Annie took her turn telling about the riding toys she'd found for pennies on the dollar. She had to use more than one hand to count how many bicycles, three wheelers, and tricycles filled our garage. It was a delight to hear that my sweet wife bragged about avoiding the hefty prices that she would have had to pay at department stores for the toys.

The three of them calculated the cash that had been saved by shopping in people's front yards instead of the aisles of big box stores. The totals were in the hundreds of dollars. As they gave each other kudos, I thought of how much money is wasted by young couples who prefer to pay top dollar for expendable things, such as toys and clothing, because they either want to impress others or they lack the gumption needed to look for better deals.

Annie later commented that the joy on the faces of her young friends as they reported such significant savings gave her hope that there are other young parents who are excited about being frugal with their funds. With that in mind she said, "If we ever have another yard sale at our house, I can add some words on our signs that might entice some of those youthful deal hunters to pull into our drive!"

Yard Sale Today!
Why pay retail when you can pay yard sale?

57

"Your Fishin' Boat Won't Sink Unless You Let the Lake In"

When I purchased our family's first motorized boat, the dealer delivered it to a dock at a nearby lake where we met him for our maiden voyage. Before he showed me how to launch, he took the time to go over some important operational features. Among the many things to remember to do was one very small item that especially got my attention. It was called the "drain plug."

Not more than three inches long and not quite as big in diameter as a 50-cent piece, the snug-fitting rubber device is designed to keep water out of the boat. It can also be removed when the boat is trailered to drain any residual water that splashes in from swimmers, skiers, fishing, or rainfall. But with that benefit comes a dangerous hazard. If the plug is not reinstalled before sailing again, it would be only a matter of time before the boat would take on enough water to cause the vessel to lose buoyancy and sink.

As spouses, we can't make each other happy, but
we can definitely make each other miserable.

Steve and Annie Chapman

With his serious warning about the drain plug, the dealer added a little story that made me shudder in fear when I thought about making the same mistake. He told of a boat owner who left the dock without the drain plug installed, got about a mile out into the lake, realized what he'd done, and in a panic dove into the water to attempt to put it in. Unfortunately he ended up at the bottom of the lake with his boat.

That story sowed enough respect for the purpose of the drain plug in my heart that I never experienced a problem because I never forgot to install it. But there was another benefit from hearing about such a tragedy that was good for me, and I'm sure you can benefit from it too. It's a character-building illustration of what can happen in our spiritual lives.

This world is like a big lake that's filled with temptations of every sort. Like it or not, each of us sets sail on the waters every day. As we do, may God help us remember to make sure the seal of His grace is in our hearts. If we fail to do so, then essentially we allow the lake to get into the boat with us. When that happens, we're bound to sink.

> Walk by the Spirit, and you will not carry out the desire of
> the flesh (Galatians 5:16).

58

"Some People Just Need Someone to Listen"

After I spoke at a wild-game dinner event, I headed to the table where my books and music were located. The organization sponsoring the event had enlisted the help of a woman to oversee the sales to allow me the freedom to greet the attendees who came by.

I had some brief and enjoyable exchanges with fellow sportsmen and sportswomen, and then a gentleman I won't forget appeared. He shook my hand and launched into a story about a big whitetail buck he'd chased for two years before finally closing the deal with his compound bow.

As he told about the successful hunt, I admit it was very interesting and quite exciting. However, he covered each detail with sentences that ran together one after another, and a line was forming behind him that was made up of several other guys who were kind enough to want to visit me and my table.

The man who had cornered me was talking so rapidly that I could hardly get in a grunt to let him know I was listening. After three or four minutes, I started feeling very concerned about the wait the storyteller was causing for those who were behind him. I began to search my mind for a way to end our conversation nicely. Nothing seemed to work. I actually thought about getting my cell phone out of my pocket, putting it to my ear, and saying, "Sorry, I gotta get this." But lying wasn't the answer—as tempting as it was.

Finally, as though the word bucket in his mind had been emptied, the fellow stopped talking, politely shook my hand, said goodbye, walked away, and blended into the crowd in the lobby.

I was exhausted emotionally and worried that it showed on my face, as I looked at the lady who was helping me with the sales. She smiled and said, "Bless your heart. You just encountered my sweet husband."

I returned her smile.

And then she sighed deeply as she added a statement that contained a ton of truth: "Some people don't need someone to talk to; they just need someone to listen."

I suppose I'll never know if a feeling of loneliness motivated the woman's husband to talk so abundantly. I wondered if he lacked male friends, and for that reason he seized the chance to corral me—a fellow hunting enthusiast—for a few minutes. I also wondered if he might have been dealing with some type of nervous disorder that drove him to talk with such abandon. Whatever the reason, I'm glad I could be there for him…and for his obviously word-worn wife.

"The Narrow Road Is Narrower Than We Think"

Some friends went to a Christmas party in the home of a fellow church member. Most of the guests were also members of the church my friends had been attending for only a few months. As they entered the foyer of the home, their hearts were warmed by the seasonal decorations, the smell of a fresh-cooked dinner, and the crackling sound of burning wood in the fireplace. But what they saw moments later caused their feelings to cool.

When they followed the hostess into a room where the appetizer table was placed, their hearts sank at the sight of what was available beside the finger foods. At one end of the table were several tall bottles of liquor and wine of various brands, colors, and flavors. Next to the bottles was a self-serve stack of shot glasses, wine glasses, and a deep ice bucket. Standing next to the offering of alcohol were some familiar faces that included the pastor, their Sunday school teacher, a member of the worship band, and the church secretary. Each of them held their personal preference of drink in their hands. They smiled as they greeted the new arrivals.

Our teetotaler friends wondered if the shock on their faces was obvious as they returned their nervous hellos to their imbibing fellow churchgoers. Each of them attempted to work through the awkward moment using small talk. The wife, however, had to try extra hard to guard her tongue due to the fact that she was especially disapproving of alcohol because of some tragic family history involving its usage. She wanted to scream, "What are you thinking?" but she managed to squelch the urge.

The evening went on, and our friends noticed that those who were drinking when they arrived were still pouring it down after the meal. They also noted that the conversations were getting progressively louder, and the laughter was swelling in volume.

When they left to go home, the party was still going strong. As they slipped out, they couldn't help but wonder if the next morning they would hear that someone among the tipsy crowd had unsuccessfully attempted to drive home. They worried about the innocent others who might encounter one of the inebriated partygoers on the highway. Along with the worry was the gloomy disappointment they felt in discovering that such dangerous liberties had been taken with alcohol consumption by folks who, in their estimation, should know better.

When the husband confided in me about his sincere concern for the excessive use of drink within the membership of the church, I gave the same response I give when I hear of other excesses that tempt us.

"First, it's true that Christ has set us free from the law, but for the sake of safety and prudence we are to temper that freedom, bearing in mind Paul's admonition to 'not turn [our] freedom into an opportunity for the flesh' (Galatians 5:13). Second, Matthew 7:14 clearly states that those of us who follow Christ must walk a narrow road. In today's culture, we've lost sight of the fact that the narrow road mentioned in the Bible is a lot narrower than we think."

> The gate is small and the way is narrow that leads to life,
> and there are few who find it (Matthew 7:14).

60

"You Know You're Gettin' Old When You Eat Cheap and Then Brag About It"

Annie and I stopped for lunch at a "meat and three" on our way back home from church. We sat down at our table, which already had menus waiting for us. We scanned the options and mutually agreed to split a meal. I ordered grilled chicken, slaw, a baked potato, and green beans. Cornbread was included, and the water was free.

When it was Annie's turn to order, she smiled sheepishly and asked, "Can we just get an extra plate?"

Even though our waitress knew the tip that a two-patron table would normally yield had probably just been sliced in half, she returned an understanding grin when she heard Annie's request. I'd like to believe we had pulled her apron over her eyes so she didn't notice what we were up to, but I could tell she was aware she was serving another pair of 55-and-older penny-pinchers.

We finished our lunch, licked our fingers, took in a few final sips of our no-extra-cost, ice-cold water, put a good tip on the table, and headed to the cashier's post. After paying the tab and making our way to the sidewalk in front of the restaurant, we were surprised to meet some friends who were just arriving. Their first question was, "How was lunch?"

I answered so fast that Annie didn't have time to take a breath and form a word.

"You wouldn't believe how cheaply we ate today! We got out of there with paying only $12, tip and all!"

We chatted a little more with our friends, got into our car, and started home. I was still glowing from having saved some cash while Annie sat on the passenger side softly chuckling.

"Whatcha laughing about, babe?" I finally asked.

The truth in Annie's answer made us both smile, and it's been repeated many times since that day—especially when we're eating out with friends: "You know you're gettin' old when you eat cheap and then brag about it."

61

"Never Start a Home Repair After the Sun Goes Down"

When I reached into the cabinet under the bathroom sink to get a towel to use for drying off after I took a shower, I noticed it felt a little damp in my hands. "Hmm," I muttered, "that's interesting." I pressed it to my face to get a second opinion. Not only could I feel the dampness, I could smell it.

I abandoned the plan for a shower, got down on both knees at the sink, and started removing everything inside the cabinet. When it was totally empty I ran my hand back along the cabinet floor and, sure enough, it felt wet. After getting a flashlight and watching the supply lines for a couple of minutes I saw the problem. The fitting at the joint where the cold water line met the shutoff valve had developed a leak.

I headed to the garage to get a crescent wrench. When I got back to the bathroom, I tightened the supply-line nut. I gave the connection another couple of minutes and saw that my attempted quick fix didn't work.

The leak was a just a single drop about every minute. I could have simply placed a small bowl under the valve handle to catch the drops and waited until the next morning to make the repair. But no, that's not how I'm wired. I went into "Me see leak right now, me fix leak right now" mode.

My "won't wait to gitter dun" attitude was driven by my unwillingness to go to bed that night knowing there was a water leak in my house. I knew I'd lay awake fearing that the line would completely let go, and while I slept the entire bathroom and bedroom would flood. So I gathered my tools and started the fix.

There was one detail about the repair that I failed to remember—or maybe I subconsciously ignored it. Starting a repair like I was facing at seven o'clock in the evening is never a good idea. And there's a really good reason for it. Parts!

Before I realized what I was doing, I'd already turned the main water line off in our crawlspace and was lying painfully contorted under our bathroom sink with wrenches in my hands. By 7:15 I had the cold water supply line off and was headed to the garage to get the spare I was sure I'd find in my "all things plumbing" bin. I was mortified when I discovered that the spare was a used line that was unfit for making any repairs. I thought I'd picked up a new one months earlier, but I obviously had failed to do so.

I shot a glance at my watch and saw that it was 7:20 PM. My heart sank with the thought that the only place that would have what I needed was the big box hardware store that was 20 minutes away. I knew if I took the time to call to see if they were open until eight I'd lose precious minutes needed for shopping. I grabbed my truck keys, told Annie where I was going, and peeled out of the driveway.

As I neared the location of the store, I was relieved to see the lights were still on. At ten minutes till the top of the hour, I ran like an NFL pass receiver through the automatic sliding doors. I carried the old supply line with me for matching up with a new one. When I got to the aisle where they were located, I frantically paced back and forth looking for the matching size. When I found the section where they were supposed to be, my hand hit my forehead in shock. The one and only item that was out of stock was the very line I needed.

I ran to the end of the aisle looking for an employee who would be available to check if there were more in stock. I assumed that because of the hour and the day I was in the store, the staffing was limited. I couldn't find a soul. I hurriedly looked around, and two aisles over I finally located some help. Just as the recorded announcement about the closing time was blasting over the loudspeakers, the gentleman who helped me broke the bad news. He was very sympathetic as he told me that there had been a run on the line size I needed. They were expecting a shipment overnight with restocking happening by mid-morning the next day.

My shoulders drooped as I left the store knowing what I would do. Not only would I need to put the old line back on and let it leak until I could do the fix the next day, I'd need to set my alarm so I'd periodically get up and check the leak to avoid liquid disaster.

As I drove back to the house I promised myself that unless our local hardware store decides to open their doors 24 hours a day, I would never start another home repair after the sun goes down. So far so good.

"If You Fight with a Pig, You'll Both Get Dirty"

While traveling to a concert in a rental car, Annie and I listened to a radio show that featured an interview with the owners of a bakery in a western state. For reasons based on their biblical beliefs, the husband and wife had refused to make a wedding cake for a same-sex marriage ceremony. As a result, they were threatened with a lawsuit based on unlawful discrimination.

Facing financial ruin due to the hundreds of thousands of dollars in fines they would have to pay, the couple chose to shut the doors of their business. Not only were they threatened with heavy fines and mercilessly bullied, but they also received promises of personal harm from individuals in the community who vehemently opposed their refusal to make the cake. Sadly, it was reported that their children were included in the threats.

As we listened to the interview, we were both saddened and disturbed by the Christian couple's story. We were sad that their livelihood had been destroyed and that they had to deal with such a crushing blow to their constitutional rights to stand on their religious convictions. We were disturbed, however, by the question that came to our minds about why they didn't dig in and fight to the bitter end for their beliefs. That's when Annie came to the rescue of our darkening emotions with an observation that is worth passing on to others, who may have asked the same question when they heard the interview.

After lowering the volume on the radio, my very wise wife said, "Do you realize what this dear couple accomplished by closing the doors of their bakery and choosing not to drag this issue through the courts? They've come out of this with the honor of not being tagged as haters. They never threatened anyone with a lawsuit, and they didn't promise to hurt anyone physically because of their faith-based beliefs. It was only the other side that did the threatening. As a result, look at who much of the nation is looking at now with sympathy."

Never doubt in the dark what God
has shown you in the light.

Author unknown

As Annie spoke, thankfully the dark clouds of anger were going away in my mind. I was all-ears as she continued.

"I can't imagine how anyone with an ounce of decency and a good sense of what's right and wrong could not feel sorrow for the bakery owners' terrible losses. Because of the unfairness and harm that has been inflicted on this poor couple, it's obvious now who is intolerant of another person's belief. Because they didn't return evil for evil or hatred for hatred, that sweet couple now has my respect for remaining unsoiled by the fight. Those who opposed them, however, are now left holding all the dirt. I'm personally proud of the bakers. They have represented righteousness very well."

Then, in reference to the mean-spirited people who had wreaked havoc in the lives of the bakers, Annie quoted something she'd heard while in high school. It was a quip that her hog-farming dad offered when he heard she was dealing with an unkind classmate. He said, "When it comes to dealing with a bully, don't forget that if you fight with a pig, you'll both get dirty."

Amen!

Never pay back evil for evil to anyone. Respect what is right in the sight of all men. If possible, so far as it depends on you, be at peace with all men. Never take your own revenge, beloved, but leave room for the wrath of God, for it is written, "VENGEANCE IS MINE, I WILL REPAY," says the Lord. …Do not be overcome by evil, but overcome evil with good (Romans 12:17-21).

"It Doesn't Cost a Dime to Dream"

It would take a lot of fingers and toes to count how many times my hunting friend Lindsey and I have stood at the edge of a particular piece of property in our home state of Tennessee and wished we owned it. The acreage we've often drooled over is made up of wooded hillsides filled with acorn-producing oaks and long, lush meadows where tasty grasses grow. It's basically a well-stocked grocery store for the large and small game that roam there.

The property is owned by people who don't live in the area, and we've heard they rarely step foot on it. Instead, it's leased to a local farmer who uses it as a place for his cattle to graze. From what we can observe as we look across the fence, there is very little human activity that happens on the grounds.

While some folks may not be drawn to such a place, Lindsey and I can't resist entertaining the fantasy of owning it. Our guess at what the acreage would cost is at least six figures, and the number at the front of the string would likely be five or higher. Assuming we'd be facing a minimum outlay of a half-million bucks for the joy of having a place of our own to chase bucks, we're forced to rely on our imaginations. The good news is, of course, it doesn't cost either of us a single dime to dream. But that could all change with a single phone call.

How tempting it is for us to do a search for the phone number of the people who hold the deed to the property and call to ask if there's interest in selling it. I wonder what we'd do if they said, "Sure thing!

—— 171 ——

I'm ready to sell." Because our longing for ownership of such an attractive and productive piece of hunting ground runs so deeply in both of us, it would be very, very hard to back out and say to the owner, "Uh, never mind. We were just dreaming."

It's sobering to think how potentially easy it would be to force our dream to come true. In this case, "buying the farm" would have a double meaning. We might end up with a nice place to hunt, but it would mean the death of our budgets and likely the demise of romance when our wives found out. So Lindsey and I will just keep on dreaming and drooling.

64

"If You Don't Sharpen Your Ax, You May Fall Before the Tree Does"

On a hot day in July, Annie and I loaded our not-air-conditioned van with two kids, luggage, toys, potty chair, highchair, playpen, sound system, and boxes of long-play record albums. We climbed into the very crowded vehicle, and the four of us headed to Texas for two weeks of concerts.

Each night and a few times during the day, we were scheduled to set up our equipment and perform. It was going to be a grueling stretch of work, but we looked forward to every opportunity to sing our songs that we'd written specifically for the purpose of encouraging families. Though it was a tiring trip I had planned, or at least I thought I had planned, the advantage of youth was on my side. What I didn't realize was what a heavy toll the constant traveling and working was taking on my health.

When you're so busy that you're not
sure if you found your rope or lost your
horse, it's time to take a serious break.

Author unknown

It was on the ninth evening of chopping away at the 14 consecutive days of traveling that I was forced to stop. Between being a busy dad, an attentive husband, a driver, the one-person road crew, speaker, singer, mechanic, and public relations manager, the rock-hard wood of responsibility had seriously dulled the ax of my health.

We took the stage that night as usual. We were 7 or so songs into a 16-song set. All of a sudden the crowd looked like a picture that was melting. I heard a low roar in my head…and that's the last thing I remember until I woke up sitting in the pastor's chair at the back of the stage.

Someone ran and got some water as Annie tended to me. Her voice sounded like she was speaking from the far end of a tunnel. When I could see clearly again, I noticed that my little audience had a collective look that seemed to be a mixture of shock and pity. They knew, as well as Annie did, that the concert was over. Being the hero that I was trying to be, however, I was yet to be convinced that the evening had ended. I fought against the idea of stopping. I didn't win the battle though, and I was escorted to the choir room for some privacy and recovery time. The pastor explained to the larger audience why the concert was over.

The next day, at the demand of my caring wife and the pastor of the church we'd shortchanged due to my exhaustion, I was resting poolside at his house with a glass of cold tea. Annie had called ahead and rearranged the event scheduled for that evening. Thanks to those who recognized that extreme fatigue had gotten the best of me, I managed to get enough rest to finish the remainder of the trip.

I learned a big lesson from that experience that I want to pass on to you. I know I have to occasionally stop "chopping" so I can sharpen my mental and physical axes through times of rest. It's a necessary thing to do. If I don't, I'll certainly fall before the tree does. Can you relate?

> [Jesus] said to [the apostles], "Come away by yourselves to
> a secluded place and rest a while" (Mark 6:31).

65

"You Choose What You Want to Do, but You Don't Get to Choose What Happens Next"

The familiar statement "Choices have consequences" seems to be lost on a particular group of people I see from time-to-time online and in the news. It's a group made up mostly of teenage boys who, as a way of getting the most hits for their video posts, do insane and body-breaking stunts, such as deliberately jumping off a garage roof and landing face-down on a concrete driveway or leaping off an object to deliberately (and painfully) straddle a wooden fence. Some have doused their clothes with lighter fluid, struck a match, ignited their shirts, and then turned fire extinguishers on themselves.

The videos that feature such craziness usually fade to black with the sound of the stunt-kid's friends laughing, pointing, and congratulating him while he moans and writhes in pain. What isn't shown is the arrival of the ambulance or, in some cases, the Life Flight helicopter, the trip to the hospital emergency room, and the weeks of recovery (assuming the injuries aren't permanent), not to mention the checks written by cash-strapped parents for medical care.

Young men who attempt to jump, cut, slam, beat, or bleed their way into the online, video-viewing hall of fame have probably heard people frantically begging them not to do those stunts. Still, the daredevils forge ahead with their plan for self-inflicted pain.

175

I have to wonder if they would reconsider if some caring person (such as one of their parents), grabbed them by their yet-to-be-broken arms and had a heart-to-heart, nose-to-nose moment with them just before they attempted to run up and over a moving car. And what truth could the loving parents share? "You choose what you want to do, but you don't get to choose what happens next."

If that type of in-the-face warning didn't make the wannabe web star stop and rethink his decision to possibly maim himself, surely the intense, fiery pain, the weeks of rehab, and the near-death experience might inspire him to never do it again…that is, if it is just a near-death experience.

66

"Good Health Is the Slowest Form of Death"

I went to our family doctor for my annual checkup. As he was tapping my knee with the little, hard-rubber mallet to see if I still had nerve endings in my leg, I quoted one of my favorite health-related lines. "Doc, someone once told me, 'If you live long enough, it'll kill you.' Wouldn't you agree?"

He offered a courtesy chuckle and said, "That's a good one, but I have one better than that."

I didn't think it was possible to top my quote, but sure enough he did.

He said with sort of a maniacal grin, "Good health is the slowest form of death."

Hearing an absolute truth like that is startling enough, but hearing it from my doctor tripled the impact. I returned a nervous laugh and didn't say much for the rest of my exam. I was too busy thinking about why I even bothered trying to treat my body with respect.

When I headed home from my yearly once over, I thought about the doc's quip and decided I would someday find a place for it in a song. Finally, I was able to use it in a lyric about the sweet anticipation that someday, thanks to God's great grace and mercy, I'll have a brand-new body that will be free from the damage time and disease have done to it.

I'm Gonna Be Brand-New

I heard about a city
Where all things will be new
And when I think of this old body
Brother, that's good news
'Cause I got things a-hurtin'
I didn't know I had
Someday when you hear I've gone there
Oh, don't be sad 'cause…

I'm gonna be brand-new…legs to go dancin'
On those streets of gold
Praisin' my sweet Savior, who died to make me whole
I'm gonna be brand-new…voice for that choir
That I'll be singin' in
To glorify the Father with a song that'll never end
I'm gonna be brand-new…it's true

I do what the doctor tells me
Eat right and get my rest
But I know that bein' healthy
Is the slowest form of death
And I know someday I'll face it
My expiration date
So I'm leaning on the promise when I
Go through those gates that…

I'm gonna be brand-new…eyes that will let me
Behold the face of God
And the beauty of His presence in that great beyond
I'm gonna be brand-new…knees that won't grumble
When I bow before the Lord
Who brought me to the place where I'll be young
     forevermore

I'll have a new body, praise the Lord, I'll have a new life!

Oh, I'm gonna be brand-new…tongue that won't stammer
When I stand and testify
'Bout all the ways He brought me through the valleys
　　of this life
Oh, I'm gonna be brand-new…ears that won't fail me
When I hear Him call my name,
"Child, enter in and say goodbye to all the pain"
I'm gonna be brand-new, I believe it's true
I'm gonna be brand-new[12]

We know that if the earthly tent which is our house is torn down, we have a building from God, a house not made with hands, eternal in the heavens (2 Corinthians 5:1).

67

"Refusing to Fear God Eventually Results in Fearing God"

In the biblical proverb "The fear of the LORD is the beginning of wisdom," the word "fear" is not a verb. It's a noun. The "fear of God" is a conviction that leads to action. For instance, if I truly believe God is all powerful, that "nothing in all creation is hidden from [His] sight" and that His eyes are "everywhere, keeping watch on the wicked and the good," then I'll be motivated to behave in ways that please Him (Hebrews 4:13 NIV; Proverbs 15:3 NIV).

What are some examples of how a sincere reverence for God influences my behavior?

- I'm be more mindful to treat others with kindness.
- I'm more generous toward the needy.
- I'm more compassionate toward the hurting.
- I'm more careful to make sure that where I go, what I see, what I say, and what I do brings honor to God.

What happens if I choose to abandon the fear of God? For one, my concern for the consequences that will impact today and eternity will fade. When there's no worry about the destruction that sin and rebellion can bring about, it's a short step to becoming prideful, arrogant, mean-spirited, greedy, perverse. From there it's a short hop to engaging in other behaviors that dishonor our holy God.

If I start down that road, the end is frightening. Its described in Isaiah 13:11 NIV: God said, "I will punish the world for its evil, the wicked for their sins. I will put an end to the arrogance of the haughty and will humble the pride of the ruthless."

Be careful what you set your heart on.
It may be the very thing that breaks it.

Author unknown

It's bad enough if I as an individual choose to deliberately dismiss the fear of God, but what happens when an entire nation does? The consequences are multiplied many times over. For example, in Old Testament times, the Israelites frequently turned their backs on the fear of the Lord, and it brought on some dreadful consequences that included 400 years of slavery in Egypt, 70 years of Babylonian captivity, and often being routed by their enemies. These results should be a warning to any nation who doesn't maintain a collective fear of God.

I'm afraid our nation won't be exempt from the same consequences if we willfully continue to neglect the reverence due our Creator. Our abandonment of the fear of God is evidenced by our lawmakers condoning the destruction of the lives of the unborn, by our society accepting the illogical and unnatural idea of same-sex marriage, and our culture's rules that continue to make prayer and Bible reading illegal acts in our public institutions and places. Sooner or later, we'll forget all the reasons we have to fear God, and then we'll suffer the terrible consequences.

The fear of the LORD is the beginning of wisdom, and knowledge of the Holy One is understanding (Proverbs 9:10 NIV).

"Some of Something Is a Lot More Than All of Nothing"

A young songwriter called to ask if I thought if it would be a good move for him to allow his song to be published by a company that had shown interest in it. During our conversation, I learned that the publisher was offering a royalty that was very close to the current industry standards. The songwriter was concerned, however, that the percentage he'd get was far less than he'd gain if he held on to the full rights to the song. I posed some questions that would help me give him the best advice possible.

"Do you own a publishing company?"

"No."

"Do you have a way to pitch the song to recording artists?"

"No."

"Has anyone else shown interest in the song?"

"No."

I paused to let the implications of my questions and his answers sink in, and then I offered the same insight I give to any songwriter who is just pulling onto the publishing highway.

"Here's the deal. Letting a publishing company represent your song is not a bad thing. If they're interested in it enough to put it in their catalog, it's a chance for you to get your foot in the door of the business. You can start your own company later."

I heard a slightly excited, "Um hmm" on the other end of the line. I sensed the idea made him both a little nervous but also hopeful.

"A publishing company has the machinery to pitch your song and get it a home with a performer or artist. That translates into product sales that generate royalty payments."

He was quick to respond, "But the company wants to take an awful lot of whatever the song makes."

I was just as quick to say, "Yes, but the company is investing their resources as well as their reputation when they pay for a demo and pitch your song. As the banker and the risk taker, don't you think they deserve a return on their investment?"

He sounded a little deflated when he said, "I suppose they do, but I could sure use a bigger percentage of whatever it generates."

In response to his concern about getting a reduced amount of royalty, I said, "Hey, man, some of something is a lot more than all of nothing!"

The writer let me know later that he made the plunge and signed the song over to the company. He was content with their aggressive and successful attempts to place the song with artists, and he was also pleased to eventually deposit his first royalty check. Much to his satisfaction, it showed a figure that was a lot more than the zero that would have been on the check if he'd written one to himself.

69

"If We Break God's Laws, They're Gonna Break Us"

A fellow once asked me, "What are the famous last words of a 13 year old?" When I answered that I didn't know he said, "Watch this!" Then he said, "But those aren't the *most* famous words of a 13 year old." I played along. "So what are they?" We both laughed when he said, "That ain't nothin'!"

The not-so-funny thing is that I can recall hearing those dangerous words used by a friend back in my younger years—just before he injured himself. We were both around the age of 13 and in the woods behind our neighborhood. We discovered a steep bank that overlooked the creek that ran through the area. We found that if we climbed up the bank about 15 feet, we could leap off and land in some soft sand that lined the stream.

For some reason, we couldn't stop ourselves from saying to each other, "Watch this!" each time we jumped. We were having more fun than boys should be allowed to have as we repeatedly climbed and threw ourselves off the ledge to land on the sand. Then, as happens so often, the challenge level dropped as we got used to the distance of the fall. That's when I heard those *most* famous words of 13 year olds.

I'd just completed another exhilarating drop into the well-stirred sand and was wiping my jeans off when my friend yelled, "That ain't nothing!" I looked up, and he'd already climbed another 15 feet higher up the bank and was preparing to leap. Apparently unwilling to settle for what had become a mild thrill, he squatted and then catapulted himself off the hillside. The outcome was not pretty.

At 15 feet, the sand was softer as it received our young bodies. At 30 feet, it mysteriously turned into the consistency of a sidewalk. When my buddy impacted the creek bank, the combination of speed, weight, and gravity caused his frame to collapse like a folding chair under a sitting elephant. His chin found his right knee, and he discovered that a jump like he tried should never be done with the tongue clenched between the teeth.

Needless to say, our morning of fun was finished as my injured comrade headed to his house. He was taken to an emergency room for stitches in his swollen tongue.

My friend had made the painful mistake of not only ignoring the law of gravity, but also trying to break it. The blood running from his mouth was plenty of evidence that he'd paid the price for his attempt.

In a similar way, when people climb the high bank of pride and attempt to break God's spiritual laws, such as do not steal, lie, or commit adultery, they need to be warned: If you break God's laws, they're gonna break you.

> Do not be deceived, God is not mocked…for the one who sows to his own flesh will from the flesh reap corruption, but the one who sows to the Spirit will from the Spirit reap eternal life (Galatians 6:7-8).

70

"We Pick Our Own Poison"

I was at mile 6 of a 12-mile run one afternoon as I trained for a half-marathon that was a few weeks away. My usual route took me on some rural back roads near our home in Tennessee, where the houses were few and far between. On occasion I would see residents out mowing their yards or tending gardens. I would wave as I jogged by their houses. There was one older gentleman in particular who saw me more than any other. One day he was at his mailbox as I approached his house. He closed the box door and waited until I was close enough to hear him speak. When I was about five yards from him he put his hand up, giving me the stop signal. I slowed down and came to a panting halt.

"How are you today, sir?" I asked.

"Oh, I'm fine, thanks. I just wanted to ask you a question."

I smiled and said, "Fire away."

He looked up and down the road and then said, "I've seen you come by here quite often. Where do you live?"

"I live about four miles from here on the other side of the highway."

"Do you run all the way from your house to here?

"I do."

The fellow raised his eyebrows as though he was impressed. "And how much further do you go out this road before you turn around and come back by here?"

I thought he sounded worried when he asked how much further it was to my turnaround point. Hoping I could ease his concern, I smiled and answered, "I go on for about 2 more miles. My goal is to do 12 miles round trip."

Then he asked, "Is there a reason you'd do such a thing?"

"Yes, sir. There are two. I do it for the exercise, plus I'm training for a race called a half-marathon. The race distance is a little over 13 miles. In order to be ready for it, I come out here this far from my house every other day."

He slowly shook his head side-to-side as he said, "Well, we pick our own poison."

That's when I realized it wasn't worry that he had for me—it was pity.

I knew I couldn't say anything to help him understand that I was actually enjoying the challenge of training for a long race, so I said, "Well, it was nice to talk to you today. I guess I'd better get on down the road."

Before I turned to restart my run, the old fellow offered one final thought.

"Young man, you do know, don't you, that about the only thing exercise is good for is to help you look good in your casket?"

Like most diehard runners would have done who didn't want to be dissuaded to pound the pavement, I laughed at his comment and put it aside.

After thirty, it's patch, patch, patch!

Jimmy Stewart

Time went by and I continued to train. I completed the half-marathon and started to train for a full marathon. Shortly after running the full marathon, about six months after talking to the elderly man, I remembered his words. It was during my recovery from the surgery required to repair the self-inflicted injury to my right knee caused by running and overuse. If I'd died on the operating table, I would've wanted the old fellow to come to my wake so he could see how good I looked in the shiny wooden box.

> Bodily discipline is only of little profit, but godliness is profitable for all things, since it holds promise for the present life and also for the life to come (1 Timothy 4:8).

Notes

1. Steve Chapman, "Love Was Spoken," Times & Seasons Music/BMI, 1991. Used by permission. All rights reserved.

2. Steve Chapman, "We Can All Do Better Than That," Times & Seasons Music, 2006. Used by permission. All rights reserved.

3. Steve Chapman, "Needed," Times & Seasons Music, 2013. Used by permission. All rights reserved.

4. Steve Chapman and Lindsey Williams, "Took a Bullet For," Really Big Bison Music/SESAC, Times & Seasons Music/BMI, 2008. Used by permission. All rights reserved.

5. Vincent Terrace, *Television Introductions* (Lanham, Maryland: Scarecrow Press/Rowman & Littlefield Publishing Group, Inc., 2014), "The Adventures of Superman," 60.

6. Steve Chapman, "Made for the Mines," Times & Seasons Music/BMI, 2009. Used by permission. All rights reserved.

7. Steve Chapman, "Play or Not," Times & Seasons Music/BMI 2007. Used by permission. All rights reserved.

8. Steve Chapman, "Run!," Times & Seasons Music/BMI, 2014. Used by permission. All rights reserved.

9. Steve Chapman and Dana Bacon, "Let 'Em Be Boys," Times & Seasons Music/Dana Bacon Music/BMI, 2014. Used by permission. All rights reserved.

10. Steve Chapman, "You Can Choose," Times and Season Music, 2014. Used by permission. All rights reserved.

11. Lindsey Williams and Steve Chapman, "You Just Never Know," Really Big Bison Music/SESAC, Times & Seasons Music/BMI, 2013. Used by permission. All rights reserved.

12. Steve Chapman, "I'm Gonna Be Brand-New," Times and Seasons Music/BMI, 2013. Used by permission. All rights reserved.